BILLIE

This Ain't No Billie Jean King Story

An Autobiography by Billie King

Edited by Vivien Cooper

Printed in the United States of America

First Printing. 2014
ISBN: 978-0-578-43668-5

201 E. Center St #112
Anaheim, Ca 92805

This book is dedicated to my mother.

I want to thank you for your unconditional love and for
allowing me to tell our story. I love you.

"Survival: A natural process resulting in the evolution of organisms best adapted to the environment."

Webster's Dictionary

A Note to the Reader

All the events portrayed in this book are factual; however, certain names have been changed to ensure privacy for all concerned.

"This image is of three survivors.
All were faced with horrific challenges and circumstances.
The one thing that kept them together was love.
I NEVER LET THEM GO."

Billie King

Foreword

How does a little black girl from a rough area of Los Angeles become linked to a white woman considered one of the greatest to ever play the game of tennis? It's all in the name.

Any time one of the elders in the neighborhood would see me coming, they would say, "Hey, what's up, Billie Jean King?"

And I would ask myself, *Who is Billie Jean King?*

All I knew was that I was born Precious King. I was a frail, lost and abused little kid who was already on the verge of a breakdown by the age of ten. I grew up in a household riddled with poverty, addiction and dysfunction in Compton, California—a city that had broken many before me.

My father, Billie King, was a handsome, robust musician. Sadly, he was also an abusive husband to my mom.

He was known and respected in the streets, notorious for his brilliance onstage as well as some unsavory sidelines that made him the kind of man you didn't want to cross in a dark alley.

I rarely saw my father but when I did, I was always in awe of him—his style, his talent, and the greatness that he exuded in all he did. I wanted nothing more than to be just like him.

When I was ten, as I began to learn more about my father, idolization turned to fear. After years of abusing and terrorizing my mother, he left us to fend for ourselves. In some odd way, despite all the violence and destruction I witnessed at his hand, when he walked out the door, he was still my hero.

With the void left by his absence, I began to get into trouble and act out. My father's peers in the neighborhood started calling me Little Billie King, saying I was just like my daddy. And at home, I was seldom called Precious anymore. I was called PK, and when I wouldn't listen, my mother would say, "There's that Billie King in you!"

Little Billie King…it started to become synonymous with me being stubborn or acting up. But for me, it meant something different. It gave this otherwise frail, frightened little girl an armor of strength that I did not feel otherwise. So, I dropped Precious and Billie became my name.

Later, my mother moved us out of Compton to Los Angeles where I was surrounded by entertainment. It was only a matter of time before I was bitten by the entertainment bug and entered the arena of music at a professional level. As I became more and more successful, nearly every interview started with the same joke: "Any relation to Billie Jean King? Ha, ha, ha!"

While completing my self-entitled book, *Billie by Billie King*, we began to do press runs, marketing and promotions. But no matter what we did, it was Billie Jean King's name that would pop up on Google instead of mine.

I kept thinking, After more than half my life fighting for a real voice, I am finally ready to tell my story, and it is being overshadowed? Seriously?

Some said, "Just use your given first name, Precious," but I couldn't. I had become Billie in every way that mattered, and especially in the way the name gave me the strength to write the book in the first place. It was truly written by Billie King.

I decided to get even bolder and changed the title to Billie King, instead of just Billie. *Then it hit me. I thought,* Wait a minute! If Billie Jean King's name keeps popping up every time someone googles my name, why don't I just subtitle the book, This Ain't No Billie Jean King Story.

That felt really right and I was firm in my decision. But then I realized that after all the years of hearing her name, I didn't really know anything about the life of Billie Jean King. All I knew was that she was a white woman who played tennis. I realized the time had come to finally find out who she was as a person, as a woman.

So, I started researching. I came across the documentary *American Masters: Billie Jean King*. As I started watching it, I was sure that the comparison between us was ridiculous. Here you have Billie Jean King, this amazing woman who fought for women's rights and became one of the greatest to have ever played the game of tennis. And on the other hand, you have this little black girl from Compton who came from a broken, dysfunctional environment.

Their stories couldn't be more different, right? Wrong.

No, this ain't no Billie Jean King story—but after a closer look, it very well could be.

BEHOLD THE
GREAT BIRD
CATCHER!

1

Beyond the Closet Door

I have just discovered Run-DMC, and I am sitting in my half-empty bedroom in front of a boom box, writing down all the lyrics to "King of Rock."

I'm the king of rock, there is none higher

Sucker MC's should call me sire,

To burn my kingdom, you must use fire,

I won't stop rockin' till I retire…

Someday I'll have a girl group just like them. I beg my older sister Nia to perform with me around the house, but she isn't interested at all. I used to get upset about her not wanting to play band with me, but Mama says that for now, I'm what they call a solo act. I try to dress the part—as much as I am able, anyway—wearing Mama's old blue sweat jacket with the two white stripes on the side. It's not Adidas, but it looks like it.

I'm also starting to write my own poems, and maybe I can turn them into song lyrics and put them to music. I have a lot to say. In fact, Mama says I have too much to say. I make up songs in the kitchen while she's cooking or in the bathroom when she's getting dressed. She says I have a great talent for coming up with lyrics for songs.

She also says I'm a lot like my father in that way—and in other ways that are less desirable. "Bullheaded!" she says, "just like your father."

I find that funny—and comforting. He's a big, strong, man with a lot of talent, and I like being compared to him.

During those rare times when my father is not being mean to Mama, he wakes up in the mornings happy. This morning he's performing solo—walking around the living room singing into his hair comb while wearing nothing but a t-shirt, his boxers, and a pair of boots. As he's performing, he does spins, sometimes getting down so low to the ground it looks like he's about to do the splits. But then he returns quickly to a straight position and spins again.

I watch in amazement, hoping I was lucky enough to get even half his talent.

"*Precious, precious, precious, precious, precious baby,*

you're mine" are the lyrics to a song he sometimes sings to me. The song is by Jackie Moore, a musician he likes, but my father's version is my favorite. It doesn't hurt that Precious is also my God-given name. He says I was the most precious thing he had ever seen. I like that, but not as much as being called Billie, after him.

Mama grabs two plastic bottles half-filled with uncooked rice and starts to shake them. She's making music, and it's beautiful. Mama tells Nia and me to hurry and grab two spoons each from the kitchen drawer. Then she shows us how to play them so they make music.

We are a band! Even Nia is having a great time—but it's short lived.

My father is putting on his shirt and pants, and I can see that he's angry. What just happened? What did I miss?

"Okay, that's enough," Mama says. "You two go into the room." Nia goes immediately.

"Mama?" I say.

"It's okay," she says, pushing me toward my room.

More than anything, I hate to leave Mama alone with him. I am afraid he will kill her if I am not there to stop him. So, whenever they fight and tell my sister and me to leave the room, I do everything I can to stay until the very last minute. I am so heavy with fear, it feels like my body has lead in it. When I finally give in and go to my room, I have to drag myself away from Mama. I shut the bedroom door slowly and sit on the edge of the bed.

Nia shakes her head, shrugs her shoulders, and turns on the TV.

With each of Mama's screams, I'm sure she's that much closer to dying, only a few feet away from my sister and me. I have knots in my stomach. *Oh, God, he's going to kill her! Somebody, please come help! Can't anyone hear?*

Now Nia and I are hiding in the closet behind a huge wooden door—a door without mercy. Close it too fast and catch your finger, and you can consider that finger dead. We're huddled together, our knees shaking and knocking against each other's. Our hands are over our ears, trying to block what sounds like our mother being beaten to death. The sound of hard breathing is muffled in my head from squeezing my ears so tightly.

Suddenly the noise stops and I ask my sister, "Is it over?"

She is slouched over, as always, with her eyes to the ground. She shrugs.

Slowly I take my hands from my ears, and hear a pop after releasing the tight squeeze on my head. Not wanting to get up from my knees, I crawl past Nia, stretch my hand up high to reach the slat and open the door. I hear nothing. Complete silence.

Leaving my big sister sitting there, hands still over her ears, I walk slowly into the living room. It's daytime, but the living room is dark. The furniture is turned over, and in the broken glass, I see a reflection of the sun coming through the torn curtain. I walk closer to Mama.

She's sitting on the floor with her lip busted and a huge bump on her forehead. She hands me the yellow phone handle so I can reattach it to the base that hangs on the side of the kitchen wall. Now I know how she got that huge bump.

God, why did this happen to her? Mama is so sweet and loving, and I can't imagine why my father would ever want to hurt her.

I always hear him say, "That Aries in you is going to get yo' ass killed!"

What Aries? I don't understand. Is that why they fight? I crawl up next to her, barely able to look into her face. She holds me tight. No tears drop from her eyes. The tears flow from mine instead. I'm sobbing for her.

At six years old, I'm the youngest, but I'm the one who always cares for Mama after Daddy does this to her. Nia may be three years older but she can't handle it. She still hasn't walked in to see if Mama is okay. My sister's fear makes her keep her distance, but mine has the exact opposite effect. I want to stay glued to Mama's side.

As Mama and I sit silently in the corner, holding each other tight, I am thinking, *God made me closer to Mama for a reason.*

~ ~ ~

The next day, we're running to my grandmother's house to get away from my father. She owns a house on Anzac Street in Compton, as well as the one next door and the one directly across the street. My grandparents moved here from Harlem in New York City, and this is the house where my mother and her two older brothers were raised.

We're not there more than a week before my father comes to try to talk Mama into going back to him.

As I listen to his words through the floor heater on the other side of the wall, I'm screaming inside my head, *Don't do it, Mama! Don't do it!*

I'm praying Mama won't give in to my father, not only because of what he's doing to her, but also because I love it here. Grandma has a big backyard with every fruit tree you can imagine—a lemon tree, an orange tree, a cherry tree, even a grapefruit tree. My grandfather, who I don't remember because he died when I was two, planted what looks like a Christmas tree on the side of the house. Mama says it's been growing since she was only six, and I can tell. It's huge!

From my position against the heater, I can see the Christmas tree through the side window. If I could just bend down a little bit more, I could see all the way to the very top.

Suddenly, Mama is telling us to grab our clothes. *What just happened?* I wasn't paying attention.

My father did it—he convinced her to return home with him. And now, we're in his money-green Cadillac driving home. As we turn off Anzac, I can still see the kids playing in the middle of the street. I sink into the seat.

The ride feels long and strange. The radio is loud, and Mama is surfing for a station like nothing ever happened. My father, with his huge Afro, is looking as big and bold as ever, as though he's in control of it all. My sister Nia is just sitting there, as usual, saying nothing.

I look at them, thinking, *They're all crazy!*

Back at our apartment on Pine Street, Nia and I drop our big paper bags stuffed full of our clothes. Then we head outside to play in the center of the apartment complex. Pine Street is no Anzac, but I still find interesting things to do.

Behold the great bird catcher! I tie a string to the end of a stick and use it to prop up the top of a cardboard box. Then I put bread in the center of the box, hold the other end of the string, and run to hide in the bushes. While the other kids run around, playing ball or something, I'm in a bush, waiting quietly for a bird to take the bait.

My sister never plays with other kids. She's standing off to the side, watching as I try to do what she thinks is impossible.

A bird lands and takes the bait. Then the moment I'm about to pull the string, a second bird lands. I've snared two birds! I look at my sister and see the anticipation on her face. I pull the string and scream, "Gotcha!"

Nia runs to me with excitement, saying, "I can't believe you caught those birds! That's amazing!"

I'm so happy to see her excited. I love my sister very much, but she's such a loner, it's hard to feel close to her sometimes.

She helps me secure the birds in the box and carry them to the house. When we get home, the birds start flying around the house, so fast that we can't catch them. *How did we let them get out?*

Mama says she can't believe I caught what she calls sparrows, those little bitty, brown birds. She's very angry—cussing and screaming—until we finally shoo the birds out the front door.

Mama orders us to wash our hands, but the hand-washing doesn't protect me from my second bout of ringworm. The first time, I got ringworm on my scalp, on the back of my head right below the hairline. Mama had to wash my hair with Tide detergent for a week to get rid of it.

I'm always finding dead birds, and playing with them or poking them with a stick. Mama calls me her wilderness girl. I may be afraid of the dark and need to sleep with a nightlight, but I'm not frightened of much wildlife. Mama even calls me to kill the spiders and scare away the mice. If I don't make it as a famous musician with my own band, I will think about being an explorer.

If I'm afraid of anything, it's a raccoon. Not just because they have those long, sharp, black nails, and the cartoons portray them as robbers and gangsters, but also because they're unafraid of humans.

Not long before I brought home the sparrows, I was in back of the apart ment building when I stumbled upon a couple of raccoons emptying the trash.

I stood there quietly watching as one shuffled through the trash while the other one stood on the lookout below. It's crazy how they always seem to travel in twos. Another day, I saw two raccoons walking slowly down the street, as if they had not a care in the world. When they got close to me, I thought I could shoo them away. After attempting that a few times, we had a stare down. They won and I walked away.

Exploring is fun. Right next door to our complex is a small motel with a telephone booth in front of it. I like to call the operator and hang up. The manager chases my friends and me out of there, saying we shouldn't be there in the first place, and we're making too much noise.

I haven't seen any of my friends since earlier and I'm bored. So, I'm at the motel, checking to see what's going on. There's the same man I saw yesterday, when Nia and I were on our way to school. We were waiting at the bus stop, and I noticed the man at the bus stop across the street. It was a really cold morning and my sister and

I were wearing big coats, but he had his pants down. I thought, *It's odd that he'd have his pants down when it's so cold outside. Isn't he freezing?*

Then he started playing with his private and looking right at us. Nia and I looked at each other with big eyes and said, "Oh, my God—look at him!" I am old enough to know that his private should be just that—private.

Now it's the next day and I see the same man in one of the rooms. He's lying on the bed with his pants off.

He calls to me, "Come in!"

"Me?" I walk inside. Curiosity is leading me into his room. I don't understand what's happening and I am driven by my desire to solve the mystery.

The man tells me to close the door behind me and I do. Then he says, "Come sit on the bed," and I do that too.

He is touching himself the way he did at the bus stop, and he has a strange look on his face. He asks me to come closer to him, so I get up from the bottom edge of the bed to move closer. I keep taking all these chances because I am mesmerized by the puzzle I am trying to piece together.

I have the mind of a detective. I am always hot on the trail of something. Often, that something is my mother. I love following every clue, going deeper and deeper, trying to get to the heart of the matter. She always asks me, "How do you always know where to find me?"

With this man in the motel room, it feels like I am inching my way along a cliff, getting right up to the edge, just to have a look over the side. Then, suddenly aware of the danger, I turn around and run frantically out the door. I am running back towards my apartment complex.

When I get close to home, I can hear arguing. From a distance, it sounds like Mama. *Oh, no! Not again!* I fly upstairs so fast, it feels like my feet hit only the first and top steps before I burst through the door. I am wondering what terrible thing is happening now, but it's just Mama with some friends, talking loudly over music, and having a good time.

Dang! Why do I always have to be feeling so on edge, with my heart beating a mile a minute? I am out of breath and overwrought. Now it's Mama's turn to wonder what's going on. "PK, what the hell is wrong with you?" Mama seldom calls me by my name. It's always abbreviated. She calls me PK. She calls my father BK.

This is an adults-only gathering, so my mother says, "Go to your room." I throw myself on the bed and pull the covers up over my head.

"You thought Daddy was here, huh?" Nia says.

She's right, of course. I fall asleep with my shoes still on my feet. I do this all the time, like a soldier who sleeps in his boots. I am on alert even with my eyes closed, never sure when I might have to get up in the middle of the night.

The next day, my friends and I see the man from the motel being arrested, thrown in the back of a cop car. *Wow, he must really be a bad person! I could have been really hurt.*

I never tell my friends what I did.

~ ~ ~

In the past few weeks since we came back home, I've only seen my father once or twice. So, things around here have been pretty quiet. Now he's here, and tension is filling the house. I can tell that Mama is angry. She's putting some ferocious energy into cleaning the house.

Nia and I are nervous.

My father is watching Mama, and I'm watching him. As she cleans, Mama is mumbling something sarcastic under her breath. It's making my father angry. *I wish Mama would stop. Can't she see she's making him upset?*

My father has a lot of hair, and as always, there is a pick stuck in his afro. He wants Mama to stop trippin' and comb out his hair for him. Sometimes he even has her scrape the dead skin from his feet. There's no way she's combing out his hair this time.

"Why don't you get the woman whose house you've been over to comb it?" she says.

That does it. He orders Nia and me to go into the other room. My sister runs but I take my time, walking slowly. My father starts after Mama, but she's too fast for him and runs out the front door. He's running after her.

I scream, "Mama!" as I'm running to the door. But just before Mama makes it to the bottom of the stairs, my father grabs her by the hair. He's so big and the strength he uses against her is terrifying.

He slams her head to the handrail, and she drops.

I run past him to reach her but I can't wake her. She is knocked out cold. I look at my father, asking for his help. He has done a powerful thing to Mama, and I see something in his eyes I've never seen before—fear. He believes he killed her this time. *Did he do it? Is she gone?*

She's slowly coming to. She can barely move. Our apartment is at the top of the stairs, right by the stairwell. My father walks back up to the apartment and vanishes inside. Mama is groggy as I get her up on her feet. We walk back upstairs and go inside. My father is in their bedroom.

Mama tells me to go to my room and close the door. I'm anything but sleepy, and anyway, I'm afraid to leave her. When I get into my room, I listen most of the night, hoping he won't hit her anymore.

It seems like I've just fallen asleep when suddenly Mama is waking us up. She tells us to grab our clothes, just like before. We jump into the car and take off, back to my grandmother's house on Anzac.

I'm excited to be back at Grandma's house, with the

fruit trees and all the kids on the block. As long as I'm with Mama and she's okay, that's all that matters. I'm happy again—until I walk into the house after playing and see my father in the kitchen, arguing with Mama. *Where did he come from?*

He is pushing Mama against the refrigerator door. My sister and my grandmother are out at the store. *What am I going to do? I have to do something, but what?*

He is such a strong man. I am frantically trying to gauge the distance between the silverware drawer and his back. Do I have to kill him to get him to stop hurting her? Maybe if I can grab a knife big enough to stab him in the back, I can get Mama out of the kitchen.

"BK!" Mama screams at my father. "She's in here. Stop!"

He turns and looks right at me, but this time he doesn't stop. That's a first. My presence usually stops him.

I decide to run three houses down to Pam's, a friend of Mama's, to get help. She'll know what to do. Pam and I run back over to the house, but we can't find my parents. They've made it all the way to the backyard.

I run outside just in time to see my father holding two bottles, and my mother holding a butcher knife. He's grabbed those huge Coke bottles my grandmother keeps on the side of the back steps. I always have to be so careful not to knock them over. Now, he's coming toward her as she backs toward the exterior wall of the house. She has a huge knife in her hand.

I hear Pam say, "I'm calling the police!" Then she runs back into the house.

No, don't leave me. Please help her! But my voice has left me and the words won't come out.

My father is trying to kill Mama next to the lemon tree where I love to play. There's my father, pushing Mama up against the house. There's me in my memory, digging under the tree for worms and roly-poly bugs. I like to put worms in a big-toed shoe and recite a riddle: "There was an old lady who lived in a shoe. She had so many children she didn't know what to do." I fill the shoe up until the worms are overflowing out of the shoe onto my hands.

Once I chased Mama all around the yard, freaking her out. I thought it was so funny.

All I can see is the tree, Mama, and the lemons on the ground. Mama has nowhere to go. My father has her trapped against the house.

Daddy! Bottles! Knives!

"Mama!" I finally scream. When she turns to look at me, he takes the opportunity to hurl both bottles at her. They crash against the house as she ducks to get out of the way. Glass flies everywhere.

"I wasn't really going to hit her," he says, walking past me.

I run and wrap my arms around Mama's waist, my

eyes tightly closed.

I open them, and I know in that instant that the lemon tree will never be the same.

~ ~ ~

My father has a habit of popping up when you least expect him. My sister is playing on the front porch. I don't even know he is around and suddenly I hear him asking if Mama is in the house. He walks in through the wide-open door as I'm playing on the floor next to my grandmother.

Grandma is so sweet and soft-spoken, she can't do much to stop him from beating Mama. Anyway, Grandma really has no idea what he's capable of because Mama hides most of the gruesome details from her.

My father speaks respectfully to my grandmother as he pushes me out of her house. He is kidnapping me. He stops at a nearby phone booth and threatens to take me away forever if Mama doesn't do what he wants. We get back in the car.

He's asking if I'm hungry, and taking me out to eat and for ice cream afterwards. We're not talking about it at all. As we surf the streets in his Cadillac, people wave and yell out *Money Five!* And just like me, they never call him by his first name. I just sit and wait with him before he drives back to Grandma's house. He's big and strong-looking but I'm scared of him for Mama—not for me. He's never whips my sister or me. In fact, he refuses to even yell at us.

When we get back to Grandma's house, Mama runs out to the car. Before unlocking the door to let me out, he says, "I love you" and kisses me on the forehead.

I say, "I love you too, Daddy. You just have to stop hurting Mommy." He unlocks the door, lets me out, and drives off.

I watch his taillights as they become blurred, and think about my parents' relationship. It wasn't always this way. There was a time when Mama looked like the happiest mother in the world. She would model all the fancy dresses he bought her, posing around the house and in front of the mirror. The house was filled with music.

I was always under her feet, waddling around her as she danced. Nia would grab her own dresses from the closet, trying to emulate her. My father and Mama would dress up all the time and go out together. My sister and

I would watch them drive away from the picture window. They seemed so happy.

Once I overheard Grandma and Mama speaking about my grandfather. They were talking about how he didn't like my father. When Mama first brought my father home, Grandfather immediately, without even shaking my father's extended hand, pulled Grandma into the other room and told her to get rid of him at once. He said it loud enough for them to hear.

"He knew a thing or two about a no-degree, young, fancy-dressed man," Grandma says.

Mama wanted my grandfather to accept my father, and refused to stick around if my father had to leave. She let it be known that if my grandfather couldn't accept my father, she wouldn't come around any-more, either. Grandma and my uncle, who was there also, were afraid they might lose Mama for good, but their fear was no match for Grandpa's stubborn, half-Irish blood. My grandfather stood his ground when it came to my father, and passed away having never shaken my father's hand.

Grandparents

That didn't stop my father from riding in the family car at the funeral. One of Grandma's nosy friends whis-pered (also loud enough for him to hear) that he had no right riding in the family car. Mama, only giving her a stern look, went on to bury my grandfather with my father by her side.

Mama can't get over him taking me that afternoon. About those hours of my absence, Mama says it was as if my father took her breath away. Mama and I have a bond that surpasses words. My family likes to say that Mama spoiled me rotten and made it hard for any of them to watch me because I cried as soon as she left the room.

Maybe it's because she slept with me on her until I was five. My father would remove me but once he fell asleep, she would put me back. They said our breathing was in sync. The odds that she will forgive him for taking me? Slim to none.

~ ~ ~

He's come back here a couple times, trying to persuade Mama that he'll never hit her again. When he calls and I'm the one answering the phone, he swears to me that it's not as bad as I think it is. He says I'm too young to understand and promises that when we come back home, things will be better.

Mama just takes the phone out of my hand and slams it down. It seems as though she is finally starting to consider what her father was trying to tell her all those years back. I don't know if we're ever going to see our father again.

He tries to use Nia and me as an excuse to come to Grandma's house. But before he can get out of the car, Mama is standing in the window with the phone in her hand, threatening to call the police. He says some mean things and returns to his car. Every time I start to feel sorry for him, I see or hear something that makes me afraid for Mama to be near him.

What is she going to do? Will she have to leave the planet to get away from him? Mama moves us into an apartment given to her by a man she is telling people is her new boyfriend. This isn't Mars, but I guess it is close enough.

It's been quiet and Mama seems happy again. She's been dancing around and decorating the apartment for weeks now. Nia and I have met him, and he's nice enough. She's happy so we're happy.

"Mama, I need money for the ice cream truck!" I yell, running out just before the truck can get away.

He's at the ice cream truck, buying the ice cream for Nia and me. "Where is your Mama?" He asks twice.

We just look at each other, not saying a word. Mama is in the house with her boyfriend, and I'm thinking, *What is my father going to do if he finds Mama's boyfriend in there?*

From where my father is standing, he notices the open apartment door. He looks inside to see her boyfriend sitting on the couch. He walks in and closes the door.

It's our fault. We left it open when we ran out to the ice cream truck. I lose my appetite and throw my ice cream on the ground. Nia and I sit together, anticipating the loud noises that will soon come from the apartment.

"Oh, my God, Nia, what is happening in there?"

The door finally opens and they walk out together—my father and my mother's new boyfriend. They get in my father's car and drive off. Mama is standing in the doorway, angry but unable to stop them. Nia and I go into the bedroom while Mama paces around for at least an hour.

When I hear someone coming in, we peek through the door. It's her boy-friend. No sign of my father. Whatever happened between the two of them, Mama's boyfriend doesn't talk about it. I hear Mama telling him that she will have to move, that there is no way to stay where we are with my father knowing our location. My father must have threatened him. Mama knows that her new boyfriend is no match for my father and doesn't want him to get hurt.

I might as well start taking my clothes out of the drawer tonight. I know Mama will be waking us up in the morning and telling us to hurry because it's time to get out of there. Good thing I didn't make many friends.

2

Money Five

We've left Compton and are now in hiding at the home of Mikhail—a Cherokee Indian who is Mama's best friend in Los Angeles. They grew up together and since Mikhail doesn't have kids, Mama made her Nia's godmother. She has her big, stinky Boxer dog, Quincy, and us.

I often wonder about the day that my daddy took me. I wonder why he didn't take my sister too. She was right there before he got to me. I mention this to a neighbor who's also a family friend and she sighs, pushing her long, straight black hair out of her face. Then she tells us that Nia is not my father's daughter. She says my father met Mama when Nia was six months old.

"Liar," I say, and follow my sister out the door.

Nia is heartbroken. With her dark skin next to our lighter skin, she always felt different but now it's worse. I want to make Mama's big, fat, ol' friend take back what she said.

Nia is telling Mama what the neighbor said to us about my father not being Nia's father. Despite being very angry with the neighbor for telling us, Mama confirms the story. It will be years before Mama is ready to reveal more details about Nia's actual father. For now, she has other revelations to share— and they are about my father.

She starts off by telling us about the age gap between her and Daddy, and then proceeds to tell us some truly shocking facts about him. For one thing, he has many other children. And he lives with another family. For six years, Mama says, she knew nothing about his other life and children. When they met, my father claimed he had only two other children. Then, for a while, Mama would believe he had seven other children. Over time, my mother would find out from other people that my father had sired a lot more than seven children.

One of my father's brothers was the first one to alert my mom to the fact that my father had more children than he was letting on. He didn't mean to spill the beans; he assumed Mama already knew. One day, Mama had gone to meet my father and was waiting outside for him but he never showed.

Her brother-in-law said that my father had to rush to the hospital because his daughter was being born.

Mama confronted my father about this new infomation and started packing to leave. He told her that she could go ahead but that she'd have to leave me behind. She stayed four more years after that.

She also tells us things that are harder for her to say— like how my father slept with Mikhail and Mama's other good friend, Carla, while she was in the hospital recovering from giving birth to me. They both confessed to her. Mikhail said it was to let Mama know what kind of man she had. Mama's reasons for telling us are the same. She wants us to know why she can't continue to be with him.

Our father treats Mama horribly, but he is very loving towards us when he's home and they're not fighting. We love him. And in some strange way, I want to be just like him. I really don't know why I do. He's a horrible person to hurt Mama like that. But out in the world, he's loved and untouchable. And when they call me Little Billie, I feel just as untouchable.

~ ~ ~

Time seems to move quickly. I'm now ten, and my sister is thirteen. Mama finds an apartment not far from her friend's house, and we move in. My sister and I take the large room in the back. Mama takes the small room, which is closet sized, in the front. We're so happy to have our own place again. I could never relax in her friend's house. I'd head to the bathroom in the middle of the night and come face-to-face with a huge, drooling Boxer dog.

Mama has not had a job this entire time but says it's only us now, so she'll look for work. She makes friends with the lady two doors down. This lady is nice enough, but she dresses weird. She wears the shortest shorts I've ever seen and she's a bit loud. After meeting her, Mama immediately starts staying out all night.

Still half asleep, I nod off, waiting for Mama to come home this night. Then, I walk into her room to check on her. She's standing in front of her dresser, looking straight ahead but pouring a glass of water onto the floor. This is strange.

"Mama, are you okay?"

Walking closer, I step on something mushy and horrible. I look down and see vomit. She's trying to pour water on it. She's drunk. Screaming, I run into the bathroom, turn the water on, and stick my foot under the faucet. My eyes are squeezed tight, not wanting to see it between my toes.

Now queasy, I head back to bed. Why is Mama acting so weird, pouring water onto the floor and looking straight ahead? She's not herself. Mama drank at times, but this is completely different.

She makes sure we get up for school the next morning and make it to the bus stop on time, but she's still a little off. My sister and I look at each other, not knowing what to think.

When leaving to go to school, Nia says, "It looks like she's on some type of drugs." This is the first time I've heard about drugs.

At school, I can't concentrate. I'm too worried about Mama. During recess, I find Nia, but she's not concerned, so I let it go. We get back home, and Mama's still in bed, sleeping. It seems like she hasn't moved all day. Her room still reeks of vomit. I open her window and ask if she's okay.

"I'm fine, BK. Just get me some water," she says. I tell her that earlier she seemed to be on drugs.

"What do you know about drugs?" Mama asks and takes a sip of water. She assures me, "I'm not feeling well—that's all." She tells me to go out and shut the door so she can sleep a little longer.

We've been home all day with nothing to eat and we're starving. There's nothing in the fridge, only an onion. No matter how many times I open that fridge, the onion isn't going to turn into a bag of groceries. But I keep doing it anyway.

Forget this! My Jamaican friend lives next door and her mom is always cooking. I'll go over there, play with them, and stay late so they have to offer me something to eat.

It's so different over here. The house is bright and full of laughter, food, and music. It's like a different world from where I live. The only thing is, I can't understand a word my friend's mom says.

"Bit adi pot soup and it shattt, Chicken yam dumpling, bayy tings."

I believe she's offering me something to eat. "Yes," I say, vigorously shaking my head.

When I climb into bed, I thank the Lord for the Jamaicans next door. I can now sleep without another night of hunger pangs keeping me up.

~ ~ ~

Mama is still staying out late and coming home messed up. Now that I know for sure that it's drugs, I can't stop worrying about her when she's out. I'm looking out the window, hoping to see her walk up to the house. We no longer have a car. We have to depend on buses for transportation. I worry that she'll miss her stop and end up somewhere else.

From the front porch, I see Mama coming down the street. "Finally!" I run outside, happy to see her.

We live on a busy street called La Brea, half a block north of Washington Boulevard, where there's a hill. We live at the bottom of the hill.

Mama's walking down the opposite side of the busy street. I figure she'll wait until she reaches the bottom of the hill and then step into the crosswalk. I'm waiting on our side. But she sees a lapse in traffic and tries to run across before reaching the bottom.

She stumbles and falls in the middle of the street. I see the traffic begin to come over and down the hill, but she just lies there. I'm running into the street, waving my hands in front of traffic to get their attention and make sure they see Mama and stop. I see smoke and hear tires skidding. A neighbor sees what's happening and runs out into the street to help me lift her.

I feel like my heart is beating out of my chest. We walk into the house, where my sister has no idea what just happened. Angrily, I tell her what happened, walk into the back room, and slam the door. I'm ten years old, but I feel like I'm eighty. I'm always nervous. My greatest fear is that something will happen to Mama and I will lose her.

My sister thinks I'm so strong, but she doesn't know that I have a huge lump in my throat every minute Mama is not home.

I'm always staring out the window, hoping to see her walk up the street. I even make up songs, singing them softly through the dusty screen, hoping that somehow she can hear it in her spirit from wherever she is... *Mama, Mama, please come home to me...* The lyrics and melody are the same each time. The thought of her hearing me gives me peace, however short-lived.

Another night waiting for Mama to come home. Every sound I hear makes me pop up from my bed with hope that it's her. "Where are you?" I say out loud, with my blanket pulled almost all the way up to my eyes. It feels safe under here and there's enough light to see when Mama walks through the front door.

I hear her coming. I pretend to be asleep so she doesn't know I stayed up all night, waiting for her. She's knocking over things, making a lot of noise. I shouldn't get up. *Stay in the bed. Help me stay in this bed, Lord.* I hear a loud crash, and jump up to see if she is all right.

"I'm fine, PK," she says, as if she knows I'm coming before I get there.

Good and drunk is what she is. I pick up the jewelry box she knocked onto the floor, help her finish undressing, and get her into bed. She kisses me on my cheek and I slowly walk back into my room.

I'm still lying in bed awake when Mama begins moving around again. Nia is sound asleep. I have to stay up in case she needs me—but I'm so exhausted. I can barely keep my eyes open. *She's okay. I can get a little sleep, just for a minute.*

"Oh, my God, Mama!" I'm running into the bathroom where the shower curtain and rod slammed down into the bathtub on top of Mama as she grabbed it to prevent her fall. It's the loudest noise I've ever heard. My heart is beating fast as I try to lift her from the bathtub.

I lie down next to her in bed. This is the only way to keep her down. This is the only way I can get some sleep.

~ ~ ~

Despite everything, I love being with Mama. I play in her tiny room just to be close to her, even while she's sleeping. This is not the case with Nia who does the opposite. We practically have to drag my sister into the room to watch TV with Mama and me.

While Mama is sleeping, I'm looking for paper to write on. I know she keeps an old yellow notebook on the side of her bed, so I grab it. It's almost full, but in the process of flipping through it to look for some blank sheets, I notice some crazy things that make me start reading from the beginning.

Mama writes about her life before she ever met someone called Money Five and she writes about how he eventually came into her life. According to Mama's notebook, some friend invited her to a local club one evening. The club announced, "The Relations!" and two brothers from Louisiana walked out in tight, one-piece, spandex, bell-bottom suits with the top zippers down, showing their muscular bodies. They were gorgeous.

She couldn't believe her eyes. As the brothers worked the stage, Mama became infatuated with one of them. She wrote that she felt as though she was the only one in the room and he was singing directly to her. She hadn't

Billie

been out for several months. She was nineteen, recently divorced and had a six month-old baby.

When the boys left the stage, Mama's friend took one of them to her table and introduced him to her. He wasn't the one she'd eyed earlier, but he was just as handsome as his brother.

They talked for the rest of the night. He told her he was twenty-seven and the eldest of seven children. She later discovered that he was actually thirty-seven and the eldest of thirteen children.

She was infatuated with his good looks and charm. Starting that night, they became an item. He was a singer and an actor who had performed in a local hit play—and as I said, he was just gorgeous. She didn't know, however, that he was also a pimp whose street name was Money Five.

"PK, put that down! What are you doing looking through my things?" Mama says, snatching the notebook from my hands.

"I was just looking for some paper."

Mama rips two blank pages out of the notebook, gives them to me, and shoves the notebook back under the mattress, pushing it even deeper under there this time.

Wow! What is in that book?

~ ~ ~

Nia is mad at Mama. For what, I don't know. She is always mad at Mama, mostly for the drinking. Still, it feels like something more is going on with my sister. She never talks about it, but she and Mama are growing further apart by the day.

I believe Nia feels that Mama favors me. It isn't that at all. I think I must love her more, and Mama can feel that. Nia is disgusted by Mama's behavior when she's drinking and pulls away while I get closer and practically stick to her. Can't Nia see that something serious is going on with Mama and she needs us?

I haven't been outside all day, and it will be dark soon. I built a cool playhouse with these huge, flat boards someone threw by the dumpster and some old blankets from the house. I have to go out and make sure none of the kids in the building tore it down.

Nope, still here. I have an old telephone and a busted TV. Now I need to find some milk crates or some bricks for furniture. I even have some of Mama's records. Who is this? Marvin Gaye. Oh, my God, she's going to kill me. I had better take this back in the house.

Who is Mama screaming at? Nia, what's going on? Mama slaps her—not once but twice—as she sits in a kitchen chair. Nia's nose is bleeding. I run to her, and I can see the shame and fear in Mama's eyes. She makes us both go into our room. Nia hasn't said what happened. She's just sitting there, wiping her nose with a tissue.

"Nia, what happened? Tell me." She just cries herself to sleep.

I sneak back outside in the middle of the night and tear down the playhouse. It doesn't seem like I should have it after this.

~ ~ ~

I wake up to the sound of Mama crying in the living room, and notice that Nia is not in her bed. Is it happening again?

Mama's on the phone, talking to my grandmother. She is crying so hard, tears and snot are running onto the floor.

I ask, "Where is Nia, Mama?" She doesn't say. She just grabs me and sobs into the phone.

I take the phone, and Grandma tells me that Nia ran away from home and is there with her. My sister showed up at Grandma's door this morning. *How did she get way over there?*

Mama asks to speak to Nia. Grandma puts her on the phone. Mama apologizes profusely. "I'm so sorry. I didn't mean it, Nia."

Nia wants to stay over at Grandma's for a while. Mama tells her she can stay the weekend, but she has to come back for school. She hangs up.

I dare to ask for the hundredth time what happened

between the two of them because no one is telling me anything. I'm upset for so many reasons right now. I know nothing, and Nia is on Anzac without me.

~ ~ ~

It's Sunday morning, and my uncle is bringing Nia home today. I hope they're bringing food. There is never anything to eat around here. I had a dream we went grocery shopping and brought back my favorite cereals—Dig'm Smacks with the green frog and Sugar Smacks with the bear—only to wake up disappointed. I tried hard to go back to sleep to see if I could eat a bowl of cereal in my dream. It didn't work.

I am hungry and bored without my sister. Even though Nia doesn't like to do much, I miss her. I get on her nerves first thing in the mornings because

I'm so loud, and she yells at me. I miss that.

I know Mama is asleep. Maybe I can sneak that notebook she doesn't want me to see. *Got it.* This time I'll take the notebook out of the room in case she wakes up. Then I'll put it back when she isn't looking.

Money Five owned Cadillacs, one of which was green with a license plate that read, *MNYFIVE*. He manipulated Mama as pimps famously do. Money Five said he loved the way Mama was kind of square and had very little knowledge of the street life. He told her he could tell she had grown up with a higher sense of morality than his other women. Mama didn't even drink beer, much less anything stronger. And she seldom used profanity.

He loved what he called her East Coast values. Mama's father was Irish and her mother was mixed, with East-and-West-Indian ancestry. Mama was raised with both parents in the household and had been sheltered. She got no advice, warnings, or anything to make her wise to hustlers and con men. She stood no chance against Money Five's silky smooth charms.

Mama was five-foot-nine-inches tall, with beautiful long legs, light skin, and brown eyes. Money Five told her that she was delicate and sweet and that a man would be lucky to have her.

Recalling the night they met—their first date—she wrote that he was a "perfect gentleman." In her naïveté, she believed she'd hit the jackpot. He began to tell her all about his life.

They had been talking for a while in the bar where they met, but she wanted to know more about this man, so she left with him. They found a motel room but not to do the usual. He didn't touch her. They talked all night about his entertainment work and his private business on the side. He told her about his female employees, who were paid daily while working for him.

He told her how it worked. They all kept a book with the clients they entertained privately. They just went on dates with men that flew in for business appointments.

He provided them with dinner dates. That's all. She knew nothing about the pimp game. After that night in the motel, he immediately started paying her rent for her. *He must really like me to do this for my baby and me,* she thought.

But he was just spinning his web to catch her. He was setting her up to be his top whore. He already had his bottom bitch (the number-one girl in his stable), but that woman was now pregnant, "probably with his child, no less," Mama wrote.

Money Five gave her the client book that woman had apparently used before she got pregnant. "It's your book now," he said to her. He knew he'd hit the jackpot if he could persuade her to go along with it. His game was too smooth to resist.

He had just two rules: no orgasms and no black men. He said that black men could get into the minds of the women, and if the women enjoyed the sex too much, they would fall in love and leave the business.

Soon, Mama went on her first "date." She met an Asian man in a hotel lobby, and they headed up to his room. He wanted more than just conversation and a meal, but because she'd been told she'd never have to take off her clothes—just entertain—she refused his advances and left. At home, she spoke to Money Five about it.

He explained, "Some men will want it. You don't have to do it, but if you do, it'll mean more money."

He was a pimp, but to her, he was much more than that—he was the man she loved. She knew about his other employees, but she figured that since they lived together and he was helping her raise her daughter, they had a much stronger connection than he had with the rest of them.

She went out with several men and provided more than dates, dinner, and conversation. It was always hard for her, and she made excuse after excuse to stay home. Guilt, shame, and remorse kept her from even looking at her mother's face during her visits. She wasn't cut out for the game, and Money Five knew it. But she was the most desirable pony in his stable; she brought in the most money.

Mama was in a club one night, waiting to meet a trick, when she saw go-go dancing for the first time. That night, after taking care of her trick, she rushed home to wait for Money Five. She told him she didn't want to sleep with men anymore; she couldn't stand their touch. Then she told him about something else that would bring in just as much money—dancing.

He was against it. He gave her a hard time and argued with her. He flat out forbade it and said she would never make what she was used to making daily. But she talked him into letting her audition for the club. She got the gig.

After seeing the money she made, he got all his girls to dance. Of course, he had much more in mind. Dancing would be the bait, and he planned to the stage, she never slept with another trick again.

Money Five quickly became possessive, a trait that had never surfaced before, even when Mama was turning tricks. He flew into jealous rages when men lusted after her while she was onstage. He wanted her to stop dancing, but she refused.

It was easier for her to control her money in this environment because Money Five could never calculate exactly how much she made—unlike turning tricks, where he took all the money. She was now somewhat in control, so he harped on her to stop dancing and told her he wanted a baby.

She didn't want another one just then and hoped he'd turn his attention to one of the other dancers working for him. She had fallen out of love with him. When she thought deeply about it, she never really was in love. He just had a way of controlling her.

After several months of going back and forth, they began trying to have a baby. She tried for more than a year to conceive, but it did not happen. They finally saw a doctor and used the thermometer

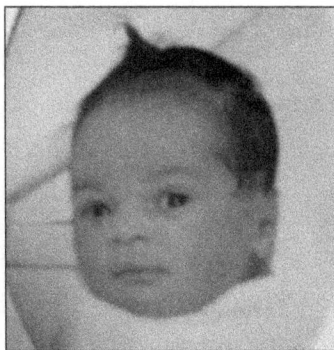

Me, 4 hours old

method. It would be a few more months before the insemination took. Nine months later, she gave birth to a daughter they named Precious King.

I drop the notebook, astonished. *My mother was a working girl and an exotic dancer? And, this pimp known as Money Five is my father?! I'm sick!*

Wait a minute—what's that on the floor? I pick up a folded piece of notebook paper, and start reading. It's by someone named Gregory Cross and at the top, it just says "Money Five."

"In the 1970s, there were mini-skirts, maxi-skirts, and afro hairdos, and all of the people were doing their own thing. Back then, you either stood out or you stood off. The Black Power Movement with its colorful Dashikis was at an all-time high. Everyone would get sharp to see the hottest acts, and the Dramatics were the group to see.

As a young buck growing up in the city of Compton, California, I had my run with gangs, guns, and drugs. But then I was turned on to a lifestyle that had a culture all its own—the fast life in the streets of fast women, where a place existed called the Razor. They called it the Razor because you had to be sharp to survive.

In my neighborhood, all the young cats loved to be clean in our tailormade suits and little pinky rings. We really thought we were the shit until one day a pretty, money green Cadillac El Dorado hit the street. It was coasting, damn near crawling, like a slow moving film, and the car's occupant had the biggest afro so perfectly in place, it was as if he had the barber in the car with him, keeping it intact.

He waved at us as if to say, "Okay, I see you little players out there." Then he stopped at the house where my beautiful homegirl lived. None of us had ever seen him over here before. As we watched him step out the car, my good friend Pete-the-Buster-the-Number-One-Hustler said, "Man, his license plates say Money Five!"

From that day forward, whenever he would come, he would have on some real fly-ass shit we had never seen before. He was always immaculate, fly, and debonair. The man was cool as the flipside of a pillow. Nails, hair, and skin were clean and always in place. Shoes were always different. I never recall seeing him in the same shit twice.

As he familiarized himself with those of us around there, he began to open up and just give us game (but not all of it). He was a suave man, and in our eyes, he had it all together. We started to emulate Money Five during our trips to the Bay Area, getting our own little piece of the street paper pie, but we just couldn't master his swag. He was a real true master at his craft and a true player. Sure, the movies had the Mack and Goldie, but we had the real deal, we had the man, we had Money Five.

That name Money Five would stick throughout the years. To this day, whenever a craps game erupts and someone gets five for a point, they'll shake the craps and holler "Money Five, money gone, Money Five money's long!" That *little rhyme came from us observing the glamorous gentle-man that we would come to know as a real cool cat.*

I am proud to have met this man, because in my entire lifetime, I still haven't met anyone like him. If God created a cooler brother, he must be somewhere in a place by himself."

~ Gregory Cross

I am totally blown away. I can't believe this is my father! Mama is still snoring softly, so I pick up the diary and continue reading.

Things got bad. They were arguing almost daily. She tried to leave the relationship, but he physically dragged her back home. She lived that life with him for six years.

No more is written in her notebook, but I start piecing together the rest of the story...Nia and me hiding

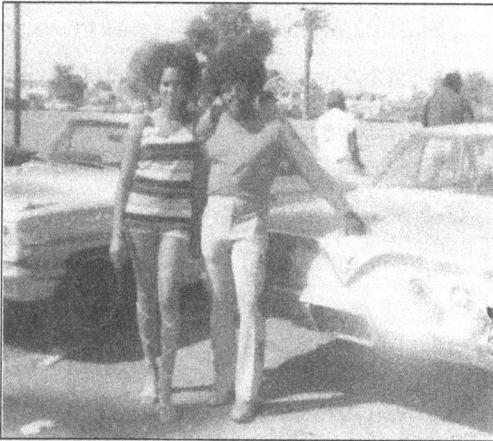

Parents

behind the closet door…running to Grandma's house… going into hiding again for two years. I often wondered why they had such a stormy relationship. After reading her diary, it all makes sense.

~ ~ ~

Mama wonders why I've been so quiet lately. Tonight she wants to watch a movie but first she says she is going to teach me how to play a card game called Tonk. We pull the dining table close to the couch and she deals the cards.

"Five for you and five for me," she says.

I'm a very fast learner, which is why she likes teaching me stuff. We play five games while listening to the Commodores and partially watching TV. Before we can finish the last game, Mama gets tired. She lies back on the couch and falls asleep.

I turn off the music so it doesn't wake her and change the TV channel. "Benny Hill. Yes!" I can't say that too loud. Mama forbids us to watch *Benny Hill*.

I'm distracted by the TV as I lean in to pick up the cards. My bangs hit the candle and now they're on fire. Mama hears me panicking and starts beating my head with her pillow. My hair is no longer on fire but my bangs are completely burnt off. Everyone always talks about my thick, pretty hair. Now I've burnt off the only thing that made me pretty.

It was scary for us both. Mama tells me it'll grow back and says not to worry. We laugh. She puts me in her arms and rocks me to sleep. This is where I feel the most secure. Here, I know she is safe with me.

I lay on her chest listening to her heartbeat. I know I'll never mention to either Mama or Nia what I've read. I'll tuck it deep and try to forget it.

3

House of Horror

I haven't seen or heard from my father in a year. I'm not sure how I feel about that. I do know that something is going on and it must be serious.

Now, Mama is talking to Grandma about us staying with my father for a little while. *I don't get it. Why would we be going to live with him?* Haven't we been running from him? I'm afraid for us to be with him because of how mean he is with Mama. But she isn't doing well—not with money, food, or other basic needs.

What is going to happen to us, to her? What if his family doesn't like us? I don't want to meet other brothers and sisters. I want to stay here. My sister and I don't seem to have any choice. We hug and kiss Mama and say goodbye.

Mama is talking to my father inside the house. She tells Nia and me, "Go wait for your daddy in the car." I am reluctant to leave them in the house alone together, but I do as she says. As I'm sitting in the backseat, tears fill my eyes.

I don't want to go. Please don't make me go. Nia doesn't want to go either. It doesn't seem to matter—no one is asking us how we feel about the move.

~ ~ ~

When we get where we're going, *You Dropped A Bomb On Me* by the Gap Band blares throughout the house. We are greeted by a light-skinned girl wearing oversized, funny-looking glasses. She's about Nia's height but a bit older.

"This is your sister," my father says, but she interrupts him before he can say her name.

"Hi. My name is Lucy," she says, being funny. Her voice is deep and hoarse like mine. Another sister and then another one come out to greet us, followed by two more. Now here comes a brother. *He looks familiar.* Daddy introduces all of them as my sisters and brother. Nia is standing there with a smile on her face.

"I can't believe you have all these sisters," she whispers to me.

I'm not so sure. It's unnerving, having all these strangers who are supposed to be my siblings suddenly smiling in my face.

Their mother, who tells us to call her Ms. Cathy, takes us to the bedrooms. I will be sharing a room with the second oldest girl. She's tall and overweight and seems to be in control of the rest of them. I can tell by the way she overpowers the conversations.

They're all older except for the one they call Lela, who's a few months younger than I am. She is so pretty. She looks like my dad, but she's light skinned like her mother. She has on a cheerleader's uniform. You can tell they are proud of her from all the pictures of her on the wall.

They live in this huge house. It's a little creepy actually. Ms. Cathy tells us to follow her upstairs where Nia will be bunking in the other Nia's room. *How weird is that? They have the same name.* Their Nia is the third daughter. She is also very pretty. She has long, pretty hair, and she's wearing a light blue bathing suit that shows off her shape. She's cool and laid back. She and my Nia are the same age. Well, I guess they are both my Nias now.

Before we get up the stairs, we pass the room my father shares with Ms. Cathy. It's just to the right of this winding staircase that leads up to Nia's room. I see a lot of pictures of my father when he was younger, along with other family photos. It's daylight outside, but it's shady on the stairs, almost dark. I try to focus on the amber light that hangs from the ceiling and illuminates the staircase, but that doesn't keep me from feeling jealous. When I see all these pictures of my father's other family, they seem like more of a real family than we do.

Before getting to Nia's room, we pass another room with a padlock. Someone inside that room is making some scary noises.

"Don't mind that noise. It's just Ruth," says Ms. Cathy. "She always stays in her room."

Who is Ruth, and why is she locked up?

Ms. Cathy explains that they have two other people living in the house, and they look after them. One of them is Ruth. Then, there's Arthur. Just as Ms. Cathy says his name, an older, grey-haired, skinny white man walks by, wearing nothing but his underwear. Ms. Cathy says, "That's Arthur."

The room where Nia will be staying is cool. It has twin beds and Michael Jackson posters all over the walls. Still, I can't help but think that in order for Nia to come in and out of her room, she will have to pass Ruth in the pad-locked room.

~ ~ ~

It's time for dinner. All of us including my father are sitting at the table, and it's overwhelming. Ms. Cathy had five girls and one boy with my dad, but Mama said Ms. Cathy also raised two of my father's boys by different mothers. One son, Sean, is here. Even though Ms. Cathy isn't his mother, he calls her Mama.

I remember him. He lived next door to us when we were on Pine Street. His mother was Mama's friend, and she was suffering with some kind of mental illness. I used to play with him, and then he vanished. One day, he was there and the next, he was gone. My father must have taken him away from his mother because she was unable to care for him.

Sean is the only one I know here, except my Nia, and it would make me feel so much more at home if he'd just acknowledge me. But, he's being standoffish. He won't even make eye contact.

My father is telling jokes, talking fast, with a little Louisiana twang. I look around the table as they all joke and laugh. When Sean starts talking about football, my father has plenty to say on the subject. I reflect back to an article Mama has, written about my father. I used to read it over and over, just trying to get to know him better.

He sang in his father's church until he was sixteen. He then started singing with quartets throughout Louisiana and Texas during his high school days. He was also a top athlete, and was offered twenty-one major scholarships from various universities upon graduation. He selected the University of Illinois, where he studied and played football for three years. He was signed by a Canadian professional football team, and continued to play professional ball for three years until a serious leg injury forced him to retire early. He and his brother teamed up as a popular singing duo, touring and recording together.

I can see some disappointment in my father's eyes as he reminisces. But instead of expressing that disappointment, he jokes that even at his age, he could run more yards than Sean.

After dinner, Lela and I play in her room. That evening, Ms. Cathy tells Nia and me that we will be checking in to school on Monday. *School? How long are they planning to keep us here?* Suddenly, I ache for Mama.

~ ~ ~

We're told that Mama is supposed to send us school clothes before the week starts. It's Monday, and no clothes. I'm forced to wear Lela's clothes and Nia wears their Nia's.

My dad isn't here that much but no one seems to mind. When he is home, he is like a superstar. The kids jump all over him. And they love hanging out in his room. I never had this kind of relationship with him. This is the first time I have seen him in this kind of family way, and I like it. Since I've been here, I've learned that he was born in Lake Charles, Louisiana, the eldest of thirteen children. That matches what it says in Mama's journal. He is the son of a Baptist preacher man (my grandfather) and a second-grade schoolteacher (my grandmother).

The sister I bunk with whispers something to me, just as I am about to enter the room my father shares with Ms. Cathy. "When Lela is in the room with them, don't you go in there."

"Okay," I say, confused.

"And don't call him Daddy," she adds.

As she sleeps, I lie there wondering how someone can tell you not to call your own dad "Daddy." *What should I call him?*

~ ~ ~

Being with my father's other family is hard on me. They hate me and they don't bother to hide it. They say they like Nia more. She's not even their sister. My relationship with my father is nonexistent at this point. I don't even speak to him because I can't figure out how to address him. If he asks me to tell one of the sisters something, how can I? What would I say? "He" says to do this or that?

"He? He, who?" I can't say "Daddy" so I just keep quiet and hope that Mama will come and get us soon. I think they're turning Nia against me too. I feel so alone.

Mama finally sends us a trunk full of clothes and Nia and I are up in her room trying on everything. I'm so excited Mama got me pink Jellies shoes and most of what we asked for. The girls come upstairs and look through our stuff. They tell Nia her stuff is pretty, but they say mine is not. I try to act as if it doesn't affect me but I can't hold back the tears any longer.

To my surprise, Nia tells them to leave me alone and to go out of the room. That is the first time Nia has defended me.

"I'm sorry," she's says. "I will never be mean to you again."

~ ~ ~

They're all out playing freeze tag. I'm shocked when they ask me to play. I'm staying close to Lela. She really likes me and wants to play with me, and when the older siblings are not focused on the two of us, we have a lot of fun together. Now we're all playing red-light-green-light, and I am really fast. I can tell they are surprised by that and because I want to impress them some more, I will try to win this game.

Lela and I are the only ones left. Now, we are racing to the finish line. I won! I won! But Lela is crying that she lost. They're all consoling her and looking at me like I did something wrong.

"Suck it up, little girl. PK was faster," my father says. *He actually stood up for me.*

Sean is congratulating me and tickling me. This makes me happy. Other than Nia, he is the only one I feel I know, and we are exactly the same because we have different mothers from the rest.

He grabs me by my hands and spins me around like an airplane. He always does it to Lela, and now he's doing it to me. Faster and faster we go, around and around. It really feels as if I'm flying. I'm laughing, and looking up at him, barely able to focus because we're going so fast. But he is not smiling back at me—in fact, quite the opposite. Then he releases my hands and I go flying. I land on the pavement, my knees and elbows scraping the ground. I'm bleeding and crying. Sean runs over, begging me not to tell. Their Nia is the one who ends up telling.

My father is furious and asks Sean why he did it. Sean shrugs his shoulders, and my father punches him twice in the chest. Sean can barely catch his breath as he runs into the house and goes to his bedroom. *Oh, my God!*

It is almost time to eat dinner, and Sean has not come down. Ms. Cathy goes up to get him, only to return with a note.

The note reads, "I hate PK. I will not come back until she is gone." They all stare at me as they put on their coats to go out and look for him.

My father, even more upset than before, stays behind. "Stop looking so sad. That boy is a knucklehead, that's all."

Nia and I go up to her room. It feels like hours before we hear them return. Their Nia walks into the room and says, "They're all mad at PK."

"Why?" My Nia says. "She isn't the one who told! You are."

Their Nia looks at us both, puts her earphones on, and lies down on the bed. My Nia tells me to go to bed and say nothing to anyone. Then she promises that this will all be better soon. I do just that, but I'm unable to sleep because of my knees and elbows stinging every time the sheet runs across them.

It's morning and Sean won't even look at me. It feels the same as when I first arrived here. All I know is that it's almost the end of the school year. Mama called and said she will come for us as soon as school is out. Please, God, I cannot spend another night in this house. Besides the fact that they hate me, there's the fact that it's scary here. For one thing, there's crazy Arthur who barely speaks, walking around in his underwear. Then there's Ruth, who I have never seen. She is still stuck behind the padlocked door. I almost got a glimpse of her, but one of the sisters slammed the door before I could get a look.

I haven't even mentioned all the rats here. They say the rats are a result of all the dairies in Compton. (Dairies are outside grocery stores where you pull up and order your food, and they bring it to you all bagged up and everything.) They say the rats go after the milk and cheese.

These rats are huge. You could be watching TV and one will just crawl up on the back of the couch and be sitting behind your head as if it's trying to watch TV too. It's not until one of the sisters yells that you know it's back there. My father is scared to death of them. It's funny to see him all big and strong and then screaming and squirming when he sees a rat. They say it's a result of something that happened when he was a kid back in Louisiana. He was going into the cupboard and as he opened it, a rat ran down his sleeve, traumatizing him.

When I hear stories like that, I feel somehow closer to him. But he is so absent. Even when he's here, he is absent.

He comes home in the wee hours of the morning wearing these elaborate clothes like he's just played a concert or something. But, thanks to Mama's journal, I know better than that. He sometimes finds me asleep on the living room floor with my back firmly against the couch. All he can see is that I'm distant from the others, but he never asks me why. He blames it on my being spoiled by Mama.

~ ~ ~

It's finally time. My father takes us back to Mama. She looks a little different now. She's thinner, but her eyes seem clearer. We throw our arms around her, feeling as if we'll never let go. They barely look at each other, but you can see that Mama is grateful to my father for taking us.

~ ~ ~

We are still having money problems and Grandma is concerned. She is living in West Los Angeles now, but she still owns her house on Anzac. The house has been empty for more than four months, and she decides that Mama should have it so she doesn't have to worry about paying the rent. I'm eleven years old and I'm back on Anzac, but this time I'm not a visitor or a fugitive. I'm here for good. *Oh boy!*

"Sometimes, she calls me the general"

4

Dizzyland

Today is glorious and I couldn't be happier. My sister and I are running through the house on Anzac, picking our rooms. We don't have any furniture yet, except for a little dining table with empty jelly jars on it, so the house echoes when we talk. I choose a bedroom in the middle of the hall. All that's in it is a twin bed that my grandma bought, with a lamp beside it. That's good enough for me. I'm excited to be here.

I've always loved Anzac, and now it's my home. My grandfather added a den and an extra room to the house. If you're standing in the living room and walk down the hall, Nia's room is on the left and mine's just a few feet from hers. Go a few feet past my room and there are three steps that lead into the den with the white tiles. To the left of the steps is Mama's room and straight ahead is the patio door.

This is where Mama grew up and she knows everybody over here. On this block, there is community. Parents died and left houses to their children, or kids just never left the nest. Either way, it's sweet home.

Anzac is a wonderful, exciting place to live. Only homeowners live on this street. It's not like all the Los Angeles and Compton apartment buildings where we used to live. There aren't many fathers on this block, just single mothers and grandmothers. But, believe me, these women don't play.

They call this neighborhood AG, which stands for Anzac and Grape (not to be confused with Grape Street in Watts). It's totally different from television portrayals of the 'hood. The block is full of kids. There are at least two children in each home, and the same is true of the homes in the next block. All the mothers on the block are quick to let us know they're not going to have us ruining their lawns or this street.

Now that we're living here, Mama is suddenly quite strict. I can't believe she won't let us go past the porch to play. I sneak down to the end of the driveway anyway and look down the street. There's so much activity. *What's going on down there?* I'm curious, but my sister doesn't care.

I'm sitting on the porch this afternoon as this fat, little girl with a short Jheri-Curl walks by. I don't remember her from our visits here. She tells me her name is Joy and tells me we're cousins. She's not sure how we're related, but I don't need the details. She's my cousin now and my buddy for life.

This is the late 1980s, and our block is called Rolling Anzac due to the fact that the block is rolling with money. One of the city's biggest drug dealers grew up on this block, and now all the teenage boys on the block work for him, hence the name Rolling Anzac. This man is a mystery to me. I can't really say I've ever seen his face because Mama won't let me walk past the porch.

Joy tells me all kinds of stories about the block, and explains how the drug game works. *I can't believe my ears. This isn't the Anzac I know!*

I tell her how I grew up in Compton and lived in this very house on Anzac when I was just a newborn. I tell her how Mama and Daddy got their first apartment together at an apartment building called The Sands, where we moved in as a family. I tell her how we lived on Oak Street, Greenleaf, K Street, Poinsettia, and Pine. I explain that the only place I've ever loved is my grandmother's house here on Anzac, where we would run and stay for weeks to get away from my father.

She tells me how she heard of my father, that the whole block has. I smile. It's then that I tell her that my family calls me Little Billie King, but she can just call me Billie. That's that—no more Precious.

Now I'm off the porch, but I can't go past the damn pink house. The block just beyond the pink house is the hangout. Joy runs back and forth, informing me about what's happening down there. I'm so jealous that she's able to see everything and I can't. I'm older. I should be running and telling her, but my mom is stricter than her mom.

~ ~ ~

It's Saturday morning, and I hear a noise outside. Joy is knocking on my door and calling my name but by the time I open it, she's already down at the end of the driveway.

"Come on!" she says.

I run and ask Mama if I can go outside. She tells me I can go if I brush my teeth first but I'm anxious to find out what's going on. I wet my toothbrush so she'll think I brushed and then I run out the door.

"He's throwing a huge block party!" Joy says. She is pointing in every direction—over here, over there—explaining that this is what the boss man does.

I see roadblocks and food trucks. The big man in charge has blocked off the whole street for a big carnival with cupcakes, snow cones, and barbecue. Mama comes out. She and her friends are eating and having a good time. Even Nia is having a good time. Did I mention how much I love it here? What a day! I can't wait to see what happens tomorrow.

The Compton I know is a place filled with fruit trees, horses, and farms. I feel like we're living in the country. I learn the hard way that I can't really climb the peach trees. They make me itch like crazy. But my friends and I raid loquat and pomegranate trees, bringing home huge grocery bags full of fruit. And we look at the horses.

After endlessly nagging Mama about letting me walk past the pink house, she finally agrees. Now she doesn't seem to worry as much about my safety in the neighborhood. None of the parents do. It's weird. There are six or seven of us who walk for blocks and as long as we stick together, our parents are cool. They are more interested in their own hobbies than in ours.

My sister doesn't hang out with us—not ever. It's not because she's older but because she's a homebody. We couldn't be more different.

One of my friends hears about a nearby farm where there are huge wild hogs, so we go looking for it. "Wow! What's that?" I ask. The smell is awful.

We hear the hogs squealing, making loud noises. We run to the wooden fence, look over, and see two huge, black hogs. I jump down immediately, scared. The size of these things excites the rest of the crew but not me. They're big enough to kill us if they could get close enough.

One boy looks for a rock or stone to throw at the hogs. He spots the top piece of a broken bottle, grabs it, and climbs back up.

"No!" I say to him, but the rest of them egg him on. Now he's up there, not knowing exactly what he's going to do.

"Scratch him on the back of his butt with it," says one of the guys in the crew.

I'm against this. The broken bottle will cut him up for sure. The hogs are in a tight, enclosed space with their backsides facing us. They can't even turn around. The boy takes the bottle and runs it fast across the hog's butt, very hard, about six times. The hog can barely move, so it's kicking and squealing loudly from the pain.

We all take off running. We're almost to the end of the block, and they're all out of breath from running and laughing. I'm not laughing. I didn't like hurting the hog.

All the older boys on the block are selling drugs. They stand on the corner, pass some drugs, and get paid. Or, they ride around in their Nissan trucks and El Caminos with Graphics and Dayton spoiler rims. Those who don't have Jheri-Curls have perms.

We sit on the curb and watch them, and sometimes we walk by with big bags of fruit. They like to chase and tease some of their little cousins in my crew. It's all in fun, but I can tell that soon the fruit trees won't be enough for the younger guys. They're ready for something bigger, ready to start making money.

I really like one of the guys in the crew. His name is Taylor. He doesn't live here but comes to visit his cousin, who lives with his grandmother, two houses from mine. I've fallen hard for this boy. He has freckles, and he's the best break-dancer on the block. He gave me my first kiss in my grandmother's garage when I was nine years old. *Wow! He's so dreamy, and he kissed me?*

Most times, I feel a little awkward. I'm taller than most of the kids in my class, and skinny, with pointy elbows and knees. And I have a hoarse voice. I'm teased at school, but on the block, even though they call me skinny, the older boys say my face is pretty. This feeds my ego.

I try to stay up on the latest fashions. I have to. This is Rolling Anzac after all, and I spend most of my time observing the game. So, I've got to look good. My sister and I are totally different in this way. She has her own style of dressing and doesn't care what people think.

For me, this is Disneyland. There's always something to get into, always something to do.

~ ~ ~

This is the era when crack cocaine gets introduced into the culture. People used to snort a little cocaine at parties but now they're freebasing crack cocaine, and that's a whole different ballgame. It's horribly addictive, and most of the parents on the block and around the corner are using and becoming addicts. This is the case with Mama, Joy's mom, my friend's mom who lives directly across the street from Joy, the mom two doors down from there, and so on. It's bad for all of us. What may have started out as harmless is now scary, hurtful, embarrassing, and dangerous.

Mama sometimes walks down the street to pick me up in front of Joy's house. Most times, she's drunk. Yes, it's embarrassing, but even with all that, she's still a sweetheart. Unlike all the other kids who say they hate their mothers when they're high, I feel I have to protect her.

Sometimes I follow her when she goes out at night. On this particular evening, she thinks we're asleep and slips out of the house. I follow her to Joy's backyard, where I see her walking into a shed. As I'm looking through a hole in the door, I see Mama light and hit the pipe—and then hit it again. She's getting high with one of Joy's relatives.

I can't stand it anymore. I bang on the door once, hard. "Mama!" I scream.

When she comes out, she's not yelling; she's not even mad at me. She comes right out and we walk home in silence. I'm sure she knows why I came, and she doesn't fight with me over it. Sometimes she calls me "the general."

Sometimes people who are high on drugs knock on the door looking for Mama.

"Hey, Billie Jean King!"

I refuse to let them in. I tell them never to knock on our damn door again, and I slam it in their faces. We have wood floors and no furniture, so when I slam that big brown wooden door, it echoes. It's just the right effect to get my point across. Then I run to my sister's room, where I can see them from her window and watch them walk down our driveway, and all I think to myself is, *Who in the hell is Billie Jean King?*

~ ~ ~

Mama left earlier this morning, and now it's ten o'clock at night and she still hasn't returned. I spend another sleepless night worrying about her. Through my sister's window, I can see just about everything going on outside. Nia's mad because I keep running into her room to see if Mama's come home.

There's Mama, standing by the lamppost! She is high and so off balance, she's unable to walk the few feet to the front door. She's rocking back and forth trying to regain her balance, and I'm watching her through the window. I don't know why I am the one who sees everything—the one who is always there. I go to help her, but when I open the door, she's already standing there, trying to put the key in the lock.

As usual, she's sloppy drunk. I don't know if I prefer one to the other, but sometimes I wish she'd just use drugs and not alcohol. I know that's an awful thing to say, but alcohol seems to make everything worse.

"Hey, PK!" she says with a slur and a smile. She seems to get sweeter when she's drunk.

Trying to stop myself from slamming the wooden door, I grip the handle tightly, grit my teeth, and close the door softly. Looking at the big smile she has on her face always calms what I feel is a beast brewing inside me. She loves me and at this moment, my heart aches for her. I take her down to her room, undress her, and put her into bed. This is always quite a task. Mama loves music, especially when she's like this. I'm trying to put her pajamas on, but she's trying to turn on the radio.

"Okay, Mama, let me do it. Lie down. I'll turn it on." Tears are welling up in my eyes. I lie down next to her in bed and throw my arm over her. I need to keep her down so she can sleep it off. She taps her feet to Tina Turner's *What's Love Got to Do with It* until she falls asleep. I'm sobbing quietly, trying not to wake her. She hears me, places her hand over mine, and then gently rubs it.

"PK...PK," she sings, trying to comfort me. Finally, she's asleep and I sneak out of bed. I'm walking back and forth, real close to the bed. I'm carefully watching her chest rise and fall to make sure she's still breathing. Sometimes it seems she forgets to breathe. Then she takes a deep breath, gasping for air. This happens so many times, I lose count. Of course, Mama won't remember any of this the next day; instead, she'll be irritable, sleeping until the late afternoon.

My sister is never in the mix. She just stays in her room while I deal with everything by myself. I wonder how two sisters born of the same mother and raised in the same household can be so different. Nia seems mean and uncaring. She doesn't seem to have the heart for Mama or for me.

~ ~ ~

Some of my best times are spent in bed with Mama, watching scary TV shows like The *Twilight Zone* or *Tales from the Dark Side*. When I was eight years old, Mama sat my cousins and me in front of the TV to watch *The Exorcist*. It scared me to death—ruined me forever. To this day, I'm afraid of the dark.

I can't sleep at all tonight. Mama isn't home, and every time I close my eyes, I hear the girl's voice from *The Exorcist*. I keep running back and forth between my room and Nia's, begging her to let me sleep with her. But she's not afraid, and she doesn't care that I am.

I've been up all night and it's almost light outside. I've got to get some sleep. I try and channel my inner Billie. My dad is not afraid of anything. I sit and try to be brave for a second, but it's not working. I sneak into Nia's room, hoping she doesn't hear me, so I can get a few hours of sleep before school. I lie down on the floor next to her bed, cautious and quiet. *Please, don't wake up,* I'm thinking to myself. Finally, I can sleep.

She's waking me up, furious. *Why? I'm not even touching her.* I can't understand why she can't let me stay here on the floor. I'm so sleepy. I crawl into my bed and sleep for what feels like only ten minutes before getting up for school.

Nia puts a lock on her door so I can't get in. That causes an issue between Mama and her. Mama wants Nia to keep more of an eye on me when she's gone—and to be nice to me. They always bump heads over me.

~ ~ ~

Things on the block are getting worse. Many parents are on a variety of drugs, and they react differently to each one. My friend Lamont's mother uses PCP. When she's on it, she strips naked in front of the whole block. This makes Lamont really angry. We try to put her clothes back on, but she fights us every time.

My cousin Joy's mother is also on PCP and other drugs. She's completely gone. Drugs affect her in the worst way—she's missing teeth and everything. She gets paranoid and thinks bugs are crawling all over her. She slaps her arms and legs and hides behind us, begging us to take them off her.

Her son, who's older, sells drugs and hates the sight of her. That's right—her dealer son is embarrassed because his user-mother is a dope fiend. He's the only dealer whose mother uses.

At first, he wouldn't allow his friends to sell to his mother, but I believe he's giving up on that difficult task.

Mama get's high and likes to wander. I spend half my time trying to keep her put. It's a trip how every crack head on the block convinces themselves they're better off than the next crack head.

Tameka's mother drives a school bus and uses drugs at the same time. But most of the time, she's a closet addict who stays in her room and smokes crack. When she gets high, she locks Tameka and her brother in the house behind their steel front door. We often sit and talk to them through the steel door. We even get locked in with them a few times.

Tameka is a girl, but she looks, acts, and dresses like a boy. They say she likes girls and they call her a bull dagger. All I know is that she can pop-lock and breakdance like a champion. She does this thing she calls the spider. *Wow, she's good!*

I admire her dance moves but I'm kind of afraid of her. She can fight—or looks like she can. Either way, she bullies me a little bit. She teases me about my flat chest and hoarse voice, so I try to stay on her good side. She also has a younger brother who's incredibly bad. I just stay away from him—period. I'm afraid he'll do something so outrageous that I'd want to knock him out. If I hit him, I'd have to deal with his sister, and I don't think I can handle her.

She and her brother have a love-hate relationship with their mother. It seems like all the kids here do, but not me. Just as I can't understand how a father could leave his kids, I can't understand kids not loving their mothers.

Don't get me wrong—there is anger inside of me. I can feel it down deep, pulling at me, wanting me to be affected by, and infected with, bitterness, evil thoughts, and sadness. I do feel that sadness, but every night and day I pray for Mama. I also pray for God to take these bad thoughts out of my mind.

I'm not being raised in a religious household at all. Mama never talks about God. She tells us to pray at night but never really shows us how. She did send us to church when we lived at the old apartment. Every Sunday, a church bus picked up my sister and me.

One day they called another little girl and me up to the altar. They begin to pray and lay hands on us. Then they're shouting aggressively. At first, it scares me. The preacher tells me to open my mouth and tell God what I want and need. I open my mouth, but nothing will come out. *Does this mean God doesn't want to hear from me?*

Their hands are pressing even harder on my forehead, almost pushing me to the ground. The other girl just leaves. I begin not to talk but to cry harder than I had ever cried before. It is as if floodgates have opened. The older ladies, who are dressed all in white and sit in the front row, surround me, and I cry myself weak.

They lay me next to Nia until the end of the service. One of the church ladies comes over to me at the end and tells me to sit up. She says that she did not like the display that went on and that she would speak to the elders about it.

She teaches me to pray by having me repeat prayers after her.

Now that I know how to pray, I can pray for Mama. "Lord, wherever Mama is, please keep her safe and bring her home to me. Amen."

~ ~ ~

Something loud awakens me from my sleep. I can hear music and I figure Mama must be entertaining someone. *Wait a minute, what is that?* I hear a loud tousle outside my bedroom. I jump up and run to see what it is. A dark-skinned man is pushing Mama around, and she's trying to get away from him.

"Mama!" I scream. "What's going on?"

She orders me back to my room. I watch from a distance as the man tries to drag Mama by her hair down the steps that lead to her room. When he sees me, he decides to drag her out the patio door instead. She's kicking and screaming. I just stand there and watch. I'm so scared, I can't seem to move for a few minutes. My heart is beating so fast, I feel like I might pass out.

I watch him drag her out the patio door, and over to the right side of the house. I run through the kitchen, open the side door, and meet them just as he gets her to the side gate. He looks up at me with a face that is dark, scarred, and pitted with craters—and he lets her go.

She runs to me, breathing hard, and I can see how badly he's frightened her. We go inside and she quickly locks the door. Then, together, we run and lock the patio door. She grabs my hand and a big knife from the drawer and we both climb into bed with Nia. With Mama holding us tight, they both fall asleep. I have many horrible visions in my head as I watch her sleep. I don't know what I would do if anything bad ever happened to her.

I never do ask her who that bad man was, or why he was trying to hurt her. He was inside our house, which means she let him in. Things must have gotten out of control. I'm guessing he wanted more than Mama was willing to give and when she refused, he tried to rape her.

~ ~ ~

I'm outside my friend's house, hanging with the crew when I see the crater-faced man who attacked Mama walking down the street. *He's coming this way!* I tell them I saw him trying to rape Mama the other night. He's very close to us now and the crew takes off after him. I'm scared, but I can still see the image of what he tried to do to Mama. In retaliation, six of my friends and I are now on his ass. We're kicking and punching him until my friend's uncle comes out and stops us.

Lamont tells his uncle what Crater Face tried to do to my mother. His uncle turns, and with a single punch, knocks the man out cold. He hits the pavement and doesn't move. We look at one another and take off running. They run home and I run to Joy's house.

Looking out her living room window, we can see him lying there. "Is he dead?"

Oh, my God! What did I do? After a few more minutes, he gets up and stumbles away.

"I bet he won't mess with yo' Mama no more," Joy says. She goes into the kitchen to get something to eat. I'm not sure I like what just happened, but she's right. I bet he won't.

~ ~ ~

Things are spiraling out of control in the neighborhood. People are OD'ing left and right. Rival drug dealers from other 'hoods are beefing with those on my block, robbing and murdering them. Some people on the block are getting killed in their mothers' houses, where they serve dope. But it's still our block, and we're growing up in the middle of it all.

Grandma is starting to ask questions about the neighborhood, thanks to Mrs. Perkins and her big mouth. She's an elderly woman who lives next door to Tameka, my friend whose mother locks her in the house. Mrs. Perkins is considered nosy, and everyone on the block hates her for it. She has a big house, a perfect lawn, and a big, clean, red Cadillac that sits in the driveway. She's mean but only to the bad kids—or so it seems to me.

I come to find out that this nosy lady is actually related to me by marriage. Her nephew, who I've known since I was born, is married to my first cousin. My sister must already know this because she's always over at Mrs. Perkins's house. I hate that Nia goes over there because it turns some of my friends against her.

Mrs. Perkins and my grandmother talk all the time. She's always telling Grandma all the bad things Mama is into. These things are news to my grandmother, who Mama always sheltered and protected from the darkness of her life. Now Mrs. Perkins is talking to Grandma about me running the streets late at night, and hanging around drug dealers. At this point, Grandma feels that it's time to sell the house and move us out of here. I look up one morning, and there's a for-sale sign in my front yard.

~ ~ ~

A loud knock echoes through the house. Joy is banging on the door, trying to get me to hurry up. First, I need to check on Mama. As I'm flying past her room, Nia looks up from some book she's reading, wondering what I'm doing.

"Mama," I call out quietly while tiptoeing over to the bed. "Mama," I call out again. I lift her eyelid to make sure she's still alive, and she wakes up a little. *Okay, still breathing.* She turns on to her side after I pull the covers over her.

Joy is standing impatiently outside but before I can get out the front door, I hear Mama yell, "Brush your teeth first!"

I run to Nia's room and, through her bedroom window, I can see Joy. She is antsy and already starting to walk away. Now she is down the driveway with two plastic bags. Just before I can get out the door, Mama is yelling for me again. Running past Nia's room for the third time, I see her laughing over my failed attempts to get out of the house.

Mama tells me to go pick something up from my aunt, who's really a good friend of hers that we call Auntie. Frustrated, I flop down on the wooden chair that sits beside her bed. All I want to do is go exploring through the neighborhood and climb fruit trees with Joy.

"What am I picking up?" I want to know.

"Don't worry about that. Just go get it." Mama says my aunt is waiting for me.

Upset, I run out the front door, slamming it behind me. The door is solid oak and the slamming of the door echoes loudly, reaching all the way to Mama's room. I can hear her screaming from here. "Stop slamming that damn door!"

I run to catch up with Joy who's already on her first tree—a loquat tree.

Her belly shakes as she jumps up and down trying to get the ripped, juicy ones at the top. I'm standing behind her, laughing at the sight. In turn, she makes fun of my knobby knees and pointy elbows. Mama says we look like Laurel and Hardy.

"Why you always making me wait?" Joy asks me. "Sorry," I say.

"Is she ok?" she asks. Joy knows what I have to deal with—she just doesn't understand why I let it affect me so. I have a stronger connection with my mom than she does. I tell her Mama is fine, but I have to go over the tracks to pick something up from my aunt's house. I can see in Joy's face that she does not want to go, for more reasons than one. Something is always happening across the tracks. I beg her to go with me but she doesn't feel like it.

Along the way, I use a water bottle to wash off the loquats. There's a spider that must have jumped off the tree and fallen onto me I'm running all over the place, begging whoever is around to get it off of me. I run into a couple who are riding two beautiful horses. I startle the black horse the woman is riding and have to take cover until she calms him down and he stops bucking. They get the horse calm and invite me to hop on.

They've taken me to Willowbrook, which will get me to the tracks. On the tracks I run into some guys I've seen before around my block. One speaks to me, then he tells me to hurry and get off the tracks. Before I can leave, some rival gang members from the other side of the tracks step to them and they start fighting. I run but only get a few feet away before I hear gunshots.

They're shooting! I'm out in the open and there is really no place to take cover. I see one drop and his side-kicks scatter. The shooter looks right at me. I run as fast as I can, trying to get to Auntie's house, but he's gaining on me.

For what feels like forever I hide in some backyard then hop a fence that will get me to my aunt's street. Where is he? Just a few feet away, I see my aunt standing on her porch waiting on me, but in the very next second I hear a gunshot. *Oh, my God! Did he shoot me?* No, that shot came from a totally different direction.

After hearing the gunshot, Auntie runs up with a friend. She's frantic and mad at me for taking so long. She puts me in the car and drives me home. When I get out, she hands me something rolled up in tissue paper. I say goodbye and walk towards home. I open the tissue and find two cigarettes. Disgusted that I went through all that for two cigarettes, I crumble them and throw them to the ground.

I'm in my bed with the cover pulled over my head when Mama comes in to check on me. She hugs me and says she's sorry that happened and grateful I'm ok. *But I'm not okay, Mama. Not at all.*

5

Darkness

The block was a fun place for me as a kid—like Disneyland. But as the other girls and I are starting to mature and develop, it doesn't feel fun anymore. These guys watch us blossom from teenyboppers into young adults, some of us blossoming more than others. Guys I grew up with are now looking at me in a whole different way. It's like they each have their sights set on certain girls, and they've made a pact to see who can get their virginity first.

They do get some of the girls by getting into their heads so much that the girls just give it up. Then the girls continue to give it up until they either get pregnant or the boys lose interest.

I never thought I'd leave Anzac, but life here has gotten completely out of hand. So many people are dying from drug overdoses and gang violence. At just sixteen, a friend who lives around the corner was shot in the head in her own bed. Her murderers were looking for a dealer she dated.

Yes, it's crazy over here right now, but this is where I discover everything for the first time. I smoke my first joint here. I drink my first beer here, given to me by my friend's older sister, who I admire and want to emulate. That same older sister also introduces me to makeup. I'm forbidden to wear it, but I sneak and do it anyway.

~ ~ ~

I'm fifteen years old, and my body is starting to fill out and feel different. I'm starting to be attracted to some of the boys on the block. Joy and I are outside and bored to death, so we go to the corner house—the dope house.

We know the guys there, so it's no big deal. We've watched them all go from taking the bus to the Roadium Outdoor Swap Meet to carjacking to driving Nissan trucks. We've watched them go from Nissans to low riders and from low riders to Mercedes-Benzes.

I'm looking through the steel front door of the dope house. I'm with Joy and our friend Stacy from around the corner. They're doing sexual things on TV, and the woman is making sensual noises. The guys in the house are not sending us away; they're letting us watch. Stacy is much more developed than we are, and she's not a virgin. She knows exactly what she's watching. I can tell just by the way she's watching it, and I feel nervous. I'm feeling my own private parts tingle and respond in ways I don't quite understand.

One of the older guys in the house comes out and makes us get away from the door. As we're walking back from the corner house and getting closer to home, I see a man in blue bike shorts and a white sleeveless tank. He has a weight belt around his waist and he's carrying a fanny pack. I'm laughing to myself. *Who in the hell is this fool?*

Then I see him taping a note to the for-sale sign at Grandma's house. *Oh, my God! It's my father! I haven't seen him in years!* He must be dressed in that strange getup because he's just come from working out.

I should have known he would find us one day. How could he ever forget the location of this house? After all, this is where he tried to kill Mama with the Coke bottles. He says he's been looking for me. *Well, okay, you found me. Now what?*

He promises to stay in touch with me. He keeps his word for a little while but not due to any effort on his part. It's Uncle Kenny, my father's brother, who makes sure I'm included in anything connected to the Kings. I'm always reluctant to go see them, but my mother pushes the issue.

Mama loves Daddy's family. She had good times with his brothers and sisters when they were younger, and they would all tease her, which cracked her up. She really

Darkness

wants me to know them. Despite my father's absence and the resentment from his other children, I really try hard to be a part of their family. But he rarely shows up anyway, so I'm quickly over it.

~ ~ ~

A new family moves onto the block from the Jordan Downs projects in Watts. It's a mother with four sons. All the girls and boys on the block are talking. The girls are checking out the new boys because they think they're cute. The drug dealers on my block are watching closely to see what these boys from Watts are up to. They could be from rival gangs, or drugs dealers from other 'hoods. No one is sure what to expect.

The second oldest in the family is Terry and he is beautiful. He's eighteen, and he looks like Michael Jackson on the *Off the Wall* album cover. All the girls like him but to my surprise, he likes me. He and Joy's brother start getting tight, and he begins selling drugs with him.

The big-timer all the dealers used to work for was murdered in his own house about four months ago. I'm hearing all sorts of horrible things about the murder. The killers tied him up, cut off his penis, and shoved it in his mouth. Now that he's gone, they work for themselves, or they work for each other, however they sort it out.

Terry, Joy, her brother, her aunt, and I are all walking down the street. Terry speaks to my cousin about me as

91

though I'm not even there. He is complimenting me, but not to my face. He wraps his arm around my neck, kisses me on the cheek, and smiles that big smile.

"When she turns sixteen, she goin' be mine," he says to everyone but me.

Wow, I'm in love.

Joy's aunt isn't much older than we are. She's just as shocked as I am that he wants me and not her. I don't dress as well as the rest of them. I'm skinny and shy around boys—not to mention the fact that I'm a virgin. This is the first time I've ever felt this way for a boy who actually feels a certain way about me.

~ ~ ~

My sister and I are starving. Mama's not home and there's no telling when she'll be back. If we have to rely on her for food, it could be a while before our next meal.

"Let's call Uncle Tee," I suggest.

Uncle Tee is the best friend of Mama's boyfriend. He must be about sixty or seventy years old. He likes to drink a bit—well, more than a bit. We've known him for many years. Sometimes he comes to our rescue when there's nothing to eat in the house because Mama's spent all the money.

Mama doesn't admit to her drug use, and she thinks she can hide it from us by lying. Whenever she spends all the money, she always claims that someone robbed her. For me, envisioning her being beaten and robbed is more terrifying than believing she spent all the money on drugs.

My sister keeps Uncle Tee's phone number, and whenever we're out of options, she calls to ask him to help us with money for food. But this time Nia is looking at me weird when I suggest that we call Uncle Tee. *Why is she waiting until the last minute to call him?*

She finally makes the call.

He takes us to McDonald's and then grocery shopping. We're eating in his car, which is parked in our driveway. I'm in the backseat, and Nia's in front, acting very standoffish. She isn't her usual quiet and withdrawn self. She seems visibly upset—like she is about to start crying. Considering that Uncle Tee just saved us from starvation, I think she could show him a little appreciation.

We finish the food, and he helps us bring the groceries inside the house. To express my gratitude, I hug him and say goodbye. He leaves.

I'm angry with my sister for the way she treated him. "What the hell is wrong with you, Nia?"

She says she didn't want to call him for help, except that we were starving. I love my sister very much and I can remember times when I felt close to her. But half the time, I just don't understand her. I'm begging her to tell me what's going on with her.

She finally starts letting it all out. She explains that he says sexual things to her and tries to touch her. Nia has always been very developed for her age. Ever since she was ten, she's been a perfect B cup. I can't understand why I have a flat chest.

"Are you *sure?*" I ask. She is sure.

"But this is Uncle Tee we're talking about. He's like sixty-plus years old!" After Nia tells me about Uncle Tee saying sexual things and trying to touch her, she tells me about Mama's boyfriend of nine years.

As she speaks, I start remembering some of it myself. It was right after we left my father for good. Nia was nine, and I was six. One night, Mama's boyfriend ran some bath water and told us to get in. Then he started taking off his clothes and stepped in with us. He told me to turn and face the back wall and told Nia to face him. I was so young, I didn't really understand what was happening. I just giggled through the whole thing.

Oh, my God, Nia! I hear her talking, but I can't get out of my own memories.

She brings up another time, her eyes filling with tears.

Yes! I remember! Her voice is drowned out by the vivid visuals flooding my memory. He climbed into our bed one night. She was facing me, and he positioned himself behind her.

"It hurts, Billie I think he's putting it in me," she had said. But at the time, I couldn't understand what she meant.

For the first time, I can really see and understand her. I understand why she's been so distant from Mama and me.

The tears fill my eyes and start to flow. "I'm so sorry, Nia. I was too young to understand what was going on."

She hugs me tightly. "I know you were," she says.

She turns to go to her room and I ask if she's going to tell Mama.

"No, that would kill her," she says and closes her door. Some years back when I came into the house and Mama was slapping Nia, it was out of frustration. Mama couldn't get any answers from her. She kept asking why she was behaving the way she was—withdrawn, distant from us, and rude to her boyfriend. But Nia just sat there, saying nothing.

Wow! Maybe that's why she's so mean. Maybe she blames me for not helping her. Maybe she blames Mama for not being there, for not knowing, as mothers should. This is her story to tell Mama, not mine. Still, I can't help but wonder what would happen if I told. I'm afraid it will push Mama over the edge. Even though her boyfriend can make her spiral further into drinking and drug use, he is the only thing that keeps her home and halfway okay. She gets lonely when he's not around.

Mama, you see, is really his mistress. He's married and has a daughter. For years, he's been promising Mama that he'll leave his wife for her, but he hasn't. If you went by her yelling at him on the phone every morning at 10 a.m. about all his broken promises and him not coming around, you'd have a hard time believing she loved him. But she lights up when she sees him. This is all sick.

~ ~ ~

Time has passed, but not much has changed. I'm still running after Mama, and Nia is still in her room, away from it all. I do have more sympathy for her, and clarity about her behavior. I used to think she didn't love or care about Mama, but it's not that at all. In her own way, she's dealing with things. She shows her love and concern for Mama by refusing to let what happened to her break Mama's heart and send her over the edge.

So, for now, things are as they are. I'm always under Mama's feet, and today is no exception. Her boyfriend and Uncle Tee are leaving, and she's walking them out. I'm in her room, setting up the scary movie we're going to watch after they leave. I'm afraid of scary movies, but Mama loves them, and I love watching them with her. Uncle Tee comes back into the room, walks up to me, and places some money in my hand.

"Put it away, and use it when you and your sister get hungry," he says. He kisses me on the lips and leaves. I'm taken by surprise but not at all afraid of him.

Uncle Tee's been around a long time. I can remember chasing him with a rubber snake, and I remember him coming over to bake cracklin' skins in our oven. We couldn't wait to pour Tabasco sauce on them, even though we were barely able to eat them because they were so hot.

He drives two Mercedes-Benzes, both red. He used to drink a lot with Mama and her boyfriend, but now all he drinks is coffee. He's short for a man, and thin. He still has a slight staggering walk as though he's been drinking, but he hasn't. He's funny and jokes a lot. He always makes me laugh.

He's at the house more and more now, even without Mama's boyfriend on the scene. He's starting to buy me things—the latest of everything. If I mention it, he'll say, "Let's go get it." He's introducing me to the finer things— things Mama can never afford. He buys me name brands like Levi's corduroys in every color, and Ellesse and Fila tennis shoes. He also buys me Turkish gold chains and earrings—whatever I want. I get my hair all feathered like Janet Jackson from the days of *Good Times.*

Mama's not always home when Uncle Tee visits. Nia starts questioning our relationship. I assure her that Uncle Tee has not touched me, but she has her suspicions and swears that he's priming me for something to come.

~ ~ ~

Uncle Tee and I are on our way back from a big shopping spree when he places his hand on my thigh. This is the first time he's done this, and I'm very uncomfortable. But I'm happy about all the clothes I just got, and besides, I'm almost home. *Wait, why is he passing my street?*

He starts rubbing my leg increasingly harder. I close my legs tight and look straight ahead, but he gets his hand between them anyway. He's rubbing the inner part of my thigh, and I can feel the side of his hand as it barely touches my private.

I'm having all these mixed feelings. On the one hand, Uncle Tee has been so good to us, and what he is doing feels interesting. At the same time, I'm nervous—and disappointed that he's doing that to me. I know Nia said he tried it on her, but why would he be interested in me in that way? I'm much younger than my sister and not nearly as well developed. I can't wrap my brain around what's happening. It's hard to accept.

I'm starting to get warm down there, but just as I start to really feel his hand where it tingles, I notice we've doubled back and pulled into my driveway. I still don't look at his face.

"Thank you," I say and get out of the car. I go inside and dump the clothes onto my bed.

Mama walks in. "Uncle Tee should not introduce you to all those things that I can't afford to buy you."

Is that all? I thought she'd be madder than this, but she isn't. She trusts

Uncle Tee, just like she trusts her boyfriend. She walks out.

I tear the tags off some pants and tops, throw on the new shoes, and head over to Joy's house. I'm hoping to run into Terry so he can see me in my new clothes. People are starting to wonder where all the new stuff is coming from, but who cares? It's none of their business.

~ ~ ~

The house finally sells, and we move off the block to a place called Fern Street in Inglewood. The apartment is okay. There are many kids my age in the next apartment building, so that's kind of cool.

Nia likes it here because it's closer to our school. Before we ever moved to Inglewood, Mama had taken us out of the Compton school district and started sending us to school in L.A. From Compton, we had to catch three buses to get to school. That meant we had to be out of the house at six in the morning to get there on time. At least now we only have to catch two buses.

By refusing to let us go to school in Compton, Mama is doing exactly what her mother did when she bused her to Los Angeles High School. I thought I had a few more years before having to leave the Compton school district—at least until high school. I was wrong.

Nia goes to school at L.A. High on Olympic Boulevard. I'm at John Burroughs Junior High down the block. John Burroughs is a stupid magnet school where they filmed *Teen Wolf* and *Nightmare on Elm Street*. It seems like some creepy school you'd find in England.

I'm terrified to walk down these scary-ass hallways. The place feels ancient and the fact that they filmed

Nightmare on Elm Street here just makes it worse. I can still see Freddy dragging Nancy's bloody body-bag down the hall, leaving a trail smeared with blood. And forget about sending me to study hall. It's in the damn basement, called the boiler room in the movie. *Are they crazy? Why did they film this here? I hate this school.*

I begin ditching school and soon I'm doing it almost every day. After a while, I can't even remember where my classes are located. I have a dream that I am searching the entire campus, walking into every classroom, but I can't find my English class. All of this is very scary, especially with the visual of Nancy's bloody body-bag in the hallway. It's horrible!

I've pretty much missed an entire semester. I forge Mama's signature over fifty times to get me back into class. Finally, I'm called into the principal's office. They hand me the phone. *I'm so busted.*

"PK, don't say anything. Do what they tell you to do, and I'll talk to you when you get home," Mama says, calmly but firmly.

I'm terrified to go home. Even though Mama is on drugs and alcohol, she doesn't play around when it comes to school. She is strict about school, like she is about many things. For instance, whenever I stuck out my tongue to tease someone when I was younger, she'd try to catch it and slap it back in my mouth. If I ever put my hand on my hip to act sexy, she threatens to break off my hip. She won't even let me wear eyeliner. When she suspects it, she wipes my eyes with a piece of tissue. If black shows up, I'm in big trouble.

The talk is going better than expected. I tell her how much I hate John Burroughs and say that if she allows me to go to school in Compton, I promise to do better. She agrees.

I start attending Willowbrook Junior High on Wilmington and El Segundo, literally a couple of blocks from Anzac. I catch three buses to go from Inglewood to Compton every morning, back and forth through some of the worst neighborhoods and the rowdiest kids. I stand on the corner of Wilmington and 103rd in Watts, close to the Jordan Downs projects.

It doesn't really affect me. Yeah, I have to watch my back, but I'm where I want to be. I get to see Joy and my other friends from the block at school every day. Mama even allows me to spend the night at Joy's on weekends and on weeknights when I have drill team practice and leave school late. Hallelujah! I'm back on the block with just a few more months left of ninth grade.

My relationship with Terry starts growing. He'd said I was going to be his when I turned sixteen years old. Well, I'm fifteen and a half now. In my heart I was his the first time I laid eyes on him.

~ ~ ~

Front 'Hood, Pocket 'Hood, and AG (Anzac and Grape) make up our 'hood. We know everybody on every block, so we're cool when we hop from block to block. Mama doesn't know this. If she did, I wouldn't be allowed to go back.

Joy lives with her grandmother and her two older aunts, but there's very little supervision. Her grandmother bolts the front door, but when she falls asleep, we take the keys out of her pocket. Her aunts aren't much better; they're usually off doing their own thing. One is dating a big-time drug dealer, and God only knows what's going on with the other one.

We sneak out and go to Pocket 'Hood almost every night. It's about six blocks from us. I make sure I don't let Mrs. Perkins see me. I don't want her ratting me out to Grandma.

I take a friend from Inglewood with me to visit Terry. I talk so much about the block that she just has to see it. We get there, and Terry is with Dave, one of the worst guys from the block. Dave's the type who does what he wants

to whoever he wants whenever he wants to do it. And no one can stop him because everyone knows he carries a gun and won't hesitate to use it.

Terry convinces me to go to a house in Long Beach with him and Dave. This house is what we call wall-to-wall plushed, all in blue. It probably belongs to some big-time drug dealer. Dave takes my friend into one room, and Terry takes me into another. I know my friend is sexually active and I'm sure she's having sex with him right now.

Terry and I talk and laugh the whole time. He only tries to kiss me once, and when he does, it's fine with me—I want to kiss him.

Dave is now in our room so he must be tired of my friend. "Okay, so now

I want some of her," he says, and closes the door.

Terry knows I'm still a virgin. Knowing Dave's reputation as a guy who takes what he wants, I'm scared. No one ever stands up to him. Terry is looking at him, not saying anything. Dave is pushing the issue. *Is Terry going to let him hurt me? Oh, my God! Are they going to pull a train on me?*

It's getting really scary in here. Where is she? How am I going to get her attention? Should I scream?

"Hell no!" Terry tells him, to my surprise. But Dave keeps trying to bully Terry into it, and they get into a huge argument. I'm looking around, trying to think of ways to get out of here. Terry pushes him out and puts the bed against the door.

"I won't let him hurt you," he says. And for the next hour, he just holds me so I won't be afraid. At this moment, there is no question in my mind how much in love I am with Terry.

6

No Way Out

I continue to go back and forth from Inglewood to Compton. Sometimes Uncle Tee picks me up in the morning to drop me off at school. Uncle Tee is getting very impatient with me. He knows I've fallen hard for a boy on Anzac, so he's becoming increasingly demanding of my time.

He's doing so much for us. Mama even asked me to see if he could help us with rent money after she messed up a couple of times. She has no idea that I have to drive around with him and let him touch me in exchange for these things.

Tonight I have a major attitude. I don't know if my love for Terry has created my newfound disgust with Uncle Tee or if it's because of his age. *No amount of clothes, food, or money is worth this.*

I meet Uncle Tee in the alley, and we drive around for a while. He puts his hand in the usual place, but he's no longer just rubbing my inner thigh. He has his hand on my vagina, and he's rubbing slowly, trying to get me to relax and enjoy it. He rubs harder and harder. I'm starting to feel warm down there.

He finds a dark street and parks the car, which usually means he wants to kiss me. I don't like kissing him. In fact, I hate it. His breath smells like coffee. He sticks his tongue in my mouth and rubs my vagina even harder. Although I'm resisting in my mind, I can feel my vagina getting wet.

He's rubbing and kissing me hard, and breathing fast—and then he abruptly stops. He has a wet spot on his pants. I didn't understand before, but I now know what that means. I care about Uncle Tee. I really do. He's been there for me. But I can't do this anymore.

"It's time to take this to the next level," he says as I exit the car. *I cannot do this. But how can I tell him without angering him, hurting him, or losing him and his support?*

~ ~ ~

The next time I see him he's overly sweet. Maybe I can find the words to tell him. Lately, though, he's been in a bad mood over the whole Terry thing. "Where are we going?" I ask.

He smiles but doesn't answer.

We pull up in front of a small white house, maybe six miles from where I live. He grabs a paper bag from the glove compartment. "Come on," he says, exiting the car.

Reluctantly, I get out. Taking my hand, he guides me to a door leading to the garage. It's dark, but sunlight seeps through the cracks in the walls and door. I see wood and dust everywhere. *What are we doing here?* I have a sinking feeling in the pit of my stomach.

He lays a blanket on the hard cement and asks me to lie down on it. Then he pulls a small bottle out of the paper bag.

"Mineral oil," he says, explaining that it's better than other oils because it won't irritate me. Suddenly, he's on top of me, between my legs. *Oh, my God! Is this happening?* He pulls down his pants and asks me to lift my butt slightly off the blanket so he can get my pants down. I'm nervous, but there's no turning back now. He tries to fit his penis into my vagina. He's very gentle, but it won't go in all the way.

"It hurts," I whisper. He kisses me softly, slows down, and tries again. "Relax," he says.

I feel his warm skin against mine as he struggles to take his time and be gentle. I focus on the rhythm of his breathing to try to loosen up, but it just won't fit. He stands and pulls up his pants.

"I don't want to force it," he says, and lifts me off the floor.

I'm not sure what I'm feeling as I pull up my pants. "Are you okay?" he asks.

I nod my head yes with somewhat of a smile. He carefully inspects me, making sure I'm completely dressed before opening the door.

The sun is bright. I feel like it's a spotlight on the wrong we've just done. He looks nervously around as we pull away. He drives me home.

Uncle Tee has been good to me throughout the years, and I do love him in my own way. I feel I owe it to him, so we keep trying. He picks me up, and we sneak into motels. I go in first, and then he follows after a few minutes. He's always making sure no one's watching. I believe we're in some kind of relationship. We go to the movies and to dinner quite often. I tell people he's my father. Uncle sounds perverted.

Despite my relationship with Uncle Tee, my love for Terry is continuing to grow. I want Terry, but Uncle Tee won't let go of me for anything in the world. I'm not even sure I want him to anymore. This weekend, Terry is showing me that he really likes me. I am overwhelmed with him, and with the fact that all the older girls like him but he wants me instead and doesn't hesitate to let them all know.

I'm at his house, lying across his bed, and we're kissing. His cousin is next to us in the same bed with another girl. We can hear him having sex with her. She's moaning and breathing quickly like the woman in that movie I was watching behind the iron door. The bed moves vigorously as he pumps her. *I can't believe they're having sex right next to us!*

Terry puts my hand on his penis and makes me touch him. I haven't felt many. *He's huge! Is this normal?* Watching his cousin and the other girl having sex in the same bed is turning him on, and he wants to be doing the same thing. He's rubbing my vagina softly while kissing me deeply with his tongue.

He puts his finger in my mouth. "Get it wet," he says, and then slides the finger inside my panties and into my vagina.

"Just do it, Terry," I whisper. He's looking at me to make sure I'm sure. Uncle Tee has touched me down there several times, but he's never put his penis all the way inside me. Terry rips his way in. *Oh, my God!* He's in and pumping hard.

"Ouch!" I feel a sharp, deep pain, and it's over. Smiling at him, I pull my panties up and walk to the bathroom.

It's tender to wipe there, and I see blood on the tissue. It reminds me of the stories I've heard about girls who lose their virginity and bleed a little. I'm smiling. I'm happy to see the blood and to know that Terry popped my cherry and not Uncle Tee.

I cannot believe that all those times with Uncle Tee we never went all the way. I know it's because he didn't want to hurt me. Terry, eager to have sex, just ripped right through me.

The very next day, I'm back at his house. We're going again, and this time, it feels like it's been going on for hours. It hurts so badly. He's pounding me and pounding me, but I don't stop him; I just bear the pain. I walk back down to Joy's house and run into one of her aunts.

"What's wrong with you?" she asks. "You're walking strange." "Nothing." I go into the house and straight into the bathroom to cry.

The next morning, my stomach is killing me. I can't even sit down or lie on my back. All I can do is lie on my side.

"PK, what the hell is wrong with you?" her aunt asks again. "Did you have sex yesterday?"

I shake my head yes, and I'm in tears.

"Was it your first time?"

"Yes."

"He hurt you," she says. "He never should've been that rough with you if he knew you were a virgin. You probably should go to the doctor."

"No! I can't. Mama can't know about this. She trusts me to be on Anzac without her, and I do not want to mess that up." And that's the end of that.

The pain eventually stops, and we continue having sex regularly. We're in love. He is so good to me. He comes to

Inglewood to pick me up and take me to the movies. We sit in the car and eat and talk about everything. I make up songs on the spot about our night, and he loves it. He tells me how talented I am and that I should do something with it.

It's hard for me to concentrate at school. I'm too busy thinking about Terry and writing lyrics for rap songs. Terry didn't graduate from high school. He tells me all the time how impressed he is with me for finishing school. So when I drift off into song lyrics or images of him, I think about that and try to concentrate on the lessons. Since he opened up to me about his feelings about not graduating from high school, I feel like I may be able to open up to him about Mama.

Now that I'm having sex with Terry, I'm denying Uncle Tee completely He is not at all happy with me, and can't understand why I keep denying him. He keeps asking whether or not Terry and I are having sex but I never answer. He takes my silence as confirmation that I am.

~ ~ ~

It's been months since I've had sex with Uncle Tee, but he still does things for me. It has turned into an uncle-niece, father-daughter relationship for real now. How weird is that? I even introduce him to Terry's mother to see if they can connect. They go out a couple of times, but I believe he's just dating her so he can stay close to me.

Joy's mom is starting to suspect that Uncle Tee is much more than an uncle to me. She is an ex-prostitute who knows all about my father. She's known me since I was a baby, so she knows that Uncle Tee is not my real uncle. I don't care what she thinks she knows. I just deny it. She's on drugs. What can she prove?

"That's PK's trick. PK knows what she's doing." She's talking to her friends like she's all for it, like she's congratulating me.

Since *she* slept with men for money, she puts two and two together in her head, and decides that Uncle Tee must be my sugar daddy—or my trick. After all, he drives those red Mercedes Benzes and has his own business. Now that she's put me on her level, she opens up even more.

She starts talking about my father being a pimp—and not just any pimp. She talks about how he had a southern flair that made him come across like a gentleman. It also made him a man who didn't stand for disrespect in any form. She says he was sharp, debonair, stylish, and tailor-made when most like him were buying off the rack. He could sing and had a body like a god. All the men wanted to be like my father, and learned how to dress by watching him. There was no woman that could resist him. He had Los Angeles and Oakland, California.

"He spoke like a preacher," she says. "He had a way of getting in deep and not letting you go even after he had let you go."

"You know you have about twenty brothers and sisters, right?" She says. "No!" *Can't she see I do not want to hear all of this?*

She doesn't stop. "Yeah, they used to say he was so potent, all you had to do was swallow it and you'd end up pregnant. Money Five," she says, and not with a happy face.

I'm so upset. I already knew he had other children. What I didn't know is that my supposed seven siblings are actually twenty—and everyone on Anzac knows it too.

While she's still talking her ass off, I'm thinking, *Since she seems to know everything there is to know about Daddy, I guess she knows everything about Mama,* too! All this time I thought I was doing such a good job of keeping it secret that Mama was once a working girl, but the older people on the block already knew. I'm ashamed, and I really do not want Terry to know any of this.

"Whatever," I say and walk away.

Joy's mom paints Uncle Tee as a dirty old man. In my heart, I believe that what started out as something dirty ended up with his love for me—and mine for him, in my own way. I want to protect him. Although we haven't been together sexually since Terry, Uncle Tee and I still go to the movies and dinner together.

This relationship is special. He's like a father to me. I know that sounds perverted, but it's true in its own way. I can hardly remember him ever touching me. All the good things he's done for me since overshadow it.

~ ~ ~

I'm seventeen now and he's sixty-eight and in poor health. I get on him about eating better. I try to get him to stop drinking coffee, but that would take a miracle. He teaches me how to drive so I can get my own car and he can stop picking me up from school.

We're moving again, this time to L.A. We're going from Inglewood back to Manhattan Place. Nia has graduated from high school, and I'm a senior at L.A. High School.

Terry and I have been together for nearly three years, but the relationship is deteriorating because of his insane jealousy. He says I am so beautiful that he can't stand for any other boy to look at me. The first time he hit me was at a red light. A car pulled up beside us and the driver was playing his music loud, so I turned and looked at him. Terry slapped me right in front of the guy. The guy was mortified, and so was I.

~ ~ ~

It's the end of senior year. Everyone is gearing up for the prom except me. I'm missing the credits I need to graduate, so I do not qualify for the prom. I don't know what I'm doing. I'm completely out of it. Terry has become extremely abusive and he's making my life hell. I am standing on the porch, looking at the girls in their beautiful gowns, all made up, walking to limousines, escorted by their dates. It's a hard thing to watch.

I cannot tell you what happened during the last part of the school year. All I know is that I was finding it impossible to focus. I was an athlete from ninth grade to twelfth, winning first-place medals and awards for excellence in running track. I'm on the drill team, and I've competed nationally. But my relationship with Terry is unhealthy, and it's taking precedence over everything.

At my school, they call him "the Iroc man" because he rolls around in his new Iroc Chevy with the ten-thousand-dollar Dayton rims. They think he's some kind of big shot. He was once sweet, the love of my life, but now he hits me for absolutely no reason.

It is 2:30 p.m. and I can see his car parked across the street on the side of the school. *What is he doing here?* The dean, who is also the football coach, says that Terry hopped the fence while they were practicing, so they had to put him out. "Be careful of him. He looks angry," he says.

Terry's car is still parked under the tree. I get into the front seat and throw my backpack in the backseat.

"Thank you for picking me up," I say, with a sinking feeling in my stomach. He is so unpredictable. As soon as I'm in the car, he slaps the shit out of me.

"What the hell is wrong with you?" I say, holding my face.

He explains that he was waiting for me at my house,

and found a letter from a boy who goes to my school who likes me. The boy is the son of the bishop at my church. As Terry is speaking, something strange happens. I hear Terry's voice, but I see my father's face.

We argue all the way to my house. I'm praying that Mama is home because this is turning into a full-blown fight.

"Bye," I say quickly. I get out and close the door, hoping he's mad enough to leave. But he's getting out and into the elevator with me. *Be home, Mama, Nia, somebody, please.* But they're not. He grabs my hair and drags me into the bedroom. I'm screaming at the top of my lungs. I hope the neighbors will hear me and break it up. He must believe someone hears me because he leaves. I swear I'll never speak to him again.

~ ~ ~

After a couple days of him apologizing and begging me to take him back, I'm at his house. *What am I doing back here?* We're arguing again, like cats and dogs. I've caught him with another girl, and now he's trying to turn it around on me.

Terry slaps me in the face repeatedly while yanking my hair. His older brother is trying to stop him but he's not trying hard enough. I can feel my hair ripping from my scalp. I pull away, running out of the house and down the middle of the street. He's not far behind me.

All this because I stood up for myself after finding out he cheated with my friend's sister. Remember the one who gave me beer for the first time and taught me how to wear makeup? The one I looked up to? Yeah, her. I run into Joy's aunts coming up the street, and Terry turns around and goes back home.

"BK, you used to be really pretty, but now you just look beat down," one of them says.

That's it for me. It's over. I never want to see him again. And this time I mean it. I ask Joy's aunts to take me home.

~ ~ ~

I have not seen Terry for a whole month, and it is not easy being without him. He was my getaway, my release. Without him around, the reality of my painful life is right in my face. One day I was in such bad shape, I threatened to throw myself in front of a school bus. Mama is on high alert, ready to call a hotline for help. It's like she has me on some kind of suicide watch. I wasn't really going to throw myself in front of a bus. It was just my dramatic way of expressing the depth of the pain I was feeling.

At least Uncle Tee is here for me. He doesn't know about the abuse I took from Terry. I protect Terry the same way I protect him. Or am I protecting myself from the shame of it all? It's hard to say. In any case, Uncle Tee is not doing too well, but he still finds the time to buy me my first car for graduation. He gives it to me even though I didn't graduate with my class. I have to attend summer school in order to get my diploma.

I haven't heard from him all day, which is unusual. I call his house, and his daughter tells me that he passed away this morning while getting dressed. She found him slumped over his bed.

I drop to the floor, struggling to breathe. His family knows about me, but they never understood why he was quite so fond of me. I believe they thought I was his daughter by another woman. Terry calls and gives his condolences. He liked Uncle Tee, who he got to know a bit when Uncle Tee went out with his mother.

~ ~ ~

I've been crying for days. I can't deal with the fact that I can no longer pick up the phone and talk to Uncle Tee. I dream that he's still alive, but then I wake up and the depression starts all over again. Before long, I start to envision him as my angel watching over me. I know that what he was doing to me in the beginning was not angelic, but there's no question in my mind that he loved me. He truly loved me, and I loved him right back.

Uncle Tee believed in me. He always told me that I was capable of anything, and I believed him. I love music, but Uncle Tee always felt that my big break would come from acting. He would say, "Once they get one look at you, they'll be hooked."

I started turning my poems into raps in the seventh grade, and he supported that before anyone else did. I've been taking rapping very seriously since I started junior high. I battled against other rappers at lunchtime and reigned supreme. But I performed my raps for Uncle Tee before anyone else.

Just before he died, he told me he was going to introduce me to his eldest son. He's the head of A&R at a major, well-known record label, and he also manages a famous rapper. Now Uncle Tee is gone, and I feel like no one believes in me. His death is extremely hard on me. I have to write about it in order to have any shot at surviving the loss. I imagine he is listening and smiling when I read what I write aloud.

~ ~ ~

Mama attends the funeral with me and Terry arrives separately. Uncle Tee was a Vietnam vet, so his casket is covered with an American flag. I remember the stories he would tell me about that time of his life. He said he lied and pretended to be of age to enlist, but he was actually just a child fighting in that war. He almost lost a toe to frostbite when he was thrown in the brig.

I can barely compose myself as Mama tries to guide me to my seat. Uncle Tee's family is looking at me. They must be wondering, who is this girl and why is she behaving like this? Uncle Tee has several grown children. One of his sons comes over to console me. *How does he know my name? I know they know about me, but as far as I know, they have never seen me.*

"Our father was very fond of you. He had several pictures of you around the house." He gives me a tissue and the program, then walks away.

"Thank you." I can't even look at the picture on the front of the program. Mama takes it and thumbs through it. "They have you in here as family, PK," she whispers.

I can't believe it. I read, *He leaves behind six children—{their names listed}, ten grandchildren—{their names listed}, a goddaughter, Billie King, and a host of friends.* They have me down as his goddaughter. He must have told them how special I was to him in order for them, who have never met me, to include me on the program.

This is all very hard to handle, and I don't know how I'll make it through to the end of the funeral service.

"We would like for you to come back to our house for the repast," one of Uncle Tee's daughters says to me. She is the one who would give me the hardest time when I called the house.

"Okay, I will. Thank you."

Mama and I thank Terry for coming and go straight home. Being listed on the program as his godchild is one thing, but that's where it's got to end. His children loved and respected their father, and actually joining them at his house as if I really was his family feels like an unkind thing to do. I will never see his family again.

~ ~ ~

I start seeing Terry again after Uncle Tee's funeral. He has been here through some of my ordeals with Mama and is now helping me get through losing Uncle Tee. In his own way, he is trying to make up for his past behavior. This is not the best relationship, but I will try and live in the moment.

I've gone through some pretty unbelievable things with Terry while also trying to escape the relationship. I've even agreed to go out of town with him on a Greyhound Bus to Sacramento. He wants me to carry some drugs. He says it's less suspicious to the police if we go as a couple.

"Now, before I die here on their bedroom floor"

7

Run, BK, Run

He has tightly wrapped several ounces of cocaine in plastic. He gives me four of them and tells me it's four ounces. I don't know anything about this stuff, but I know it's risky and I could go to jail if we get caught. For some reason, I'm not afraid.

We're wearing oversized, matching Georgetown starter jackets. He shoves two of the plastic packages in each of my sleeves, and we head to the bus station. As we board the bus with mostly old, white people, we're hugged up, acting like an innocent, loving, young couple. We head to the back and find a double bucket seat where we can sit close together.

Terry falls asleep on my lap while I stare into the night through the dark windows, able to see only the red and green streetlights and storefront signs. The smooth rocking of the bus gives me a relaxed feeling. I miss Uncle Tee. Without him around, I feel like I'm alone with no one to turn to.

I know I shouldn't be here with this person who hits me and has spit in my face before. I don't even know if I still love him. But I have lost one person already, and losing him right now would mean I have absolutely no one at all to turn to. Terry has apologized a million times for hitting me, and he claims to love me with all his heart. I saw my father do the same thing to my mother, all while saying, "I love you."

After a two-hour ride, Terry's cousin, who lives with him back in Compton, is here to pick us up at the bus station. About six months earlier, they had set up shop in a Sacramento apartment building where his aunt lives. She knows exactly what they are doing out here. I believe she is the one who set up the operation.

At first I thought it was no big deal, a small operation. When we get to the apartment, it seems like half the boys from my block start appearing from various rooms. Terry has it all figured out. He is the boss. Dave is here, taking orders. Well, not orders. I know Terry is mean to me sometimes, but all the guys on the block see him as the good guy, the cool one, because he is nonconfrontational.

"We will stay here a week," he says, "then head back." Mama knows I'm here with him, but of course she doesn't know what Terry does on the street. She feels the same way about him as the guys on the block.

We have been here two days, and I am ready to go. Honestly, I don't like being around all these drugs. I see them cook it up and cut it up, and I see the people who buy it from them. There is a woman who reminds me of Mama with a little boy of about six. Whenever she comes around, I immediately get sad and a little bit angry that Terry doesn't care who he sells to. Some of the guys are even mean to her.

I want to go home. After a shower, I try to figure out how I'm going to tell Terry I'm ready to go. He comes into the bathroom and tells me that he feels sorry for that woman, and is no longer going to sell drugs to her. I am pleased that the protective guy who prevented Dave from raping me all those years ago is still inside him. We go lay across the bed and fall asleep in each other's arms.

I've been away from Mama for six days, and I'm really worried about her. I would have been back home by now, but something big has happened, and it doesn't sound good.

"We can't leave," Terry says.

~ ~ ~

What in the world is going on? We are being awakened by police officers with guns drawn. They make us get out of the bed, then take us into the living room where they have the rest of the guys in handcuffs. I am wearing only Terry's t-shirt. Terry asks them if they could at least allow me to put on some pants.

"All these dudes in here can see her underwear," he says. He is concerned but even now, his insane jealousy is apparent. He doesn't want me looking at anyone or anyone looking at me. They bring me a towel and wrap it around my waist. Terry tells them to let me go. He explains that he brought me here unaware of what he was doing, and I had nothing at all to do with what is going on.

They take us all down to the station, but they don't throw me in lockup with the rest. An officer sits me down in a chair to ask me a few questions. Then he says they called my mother to come get me. *How is Mama going to get me? Yeah, right! You might as well throw me in with the rest. She has no money to get all the way out here.*

Six hours later, she walks through the door with her boyfriend. She signs a few papers and they release me to her. She is so angry, but she is barely speaking. "What the Goddamn hell are you doing around drugs, girl?" She finally lets it out.

I say nothing. There is no good answer to that question. I hope she can see by my intense stare into her eyes that I will never, ever see him again.

~ ~ ~

It's been a little over two months. Terry's mom went up north to go to court for him. It is possible that he could be released. I hope so for his sake, but I can't see him anymore. I hate drugs—especially what I have seen them do to Mama over the years. I'm glad that Terry and I no longer live on the same street. I don't think he is going to let me go that easily.

They release Terry, and he's back at home, begging me to come see him. Today I will, but only because he is a loose cannon and I have to let him down easy so he will leave me alone. If I do it harshly, he will never let it go.

I am happy to see that he is at home and doing well. He tells me stories about jail. Some are funny, such as the drop-and-flush rule, and some are just downright scary. He tells me that some guys are after him for the money he owes them, and he believes they saw me at the apartment so they know who I am.

"What are you telling me this for? Are you trying to scare me?"

Terry says that he just thought I should know.

Okay, I am officially freaked out on so many levels.

He says that even though we're back in L.A., they can still find us. The guys who are after him have people out here to handle their business for them.

So what do I have to do with this?

I have to take the bus back to Inglewood, so I want to leave before dark. Terry is trying not to hear that. He is asking me to spend the night.

"I can't," I say, but he insists. I call Mama, tell her not to be mad, and promise to come home in the morning. "I do not want to upset him. Give me tonight to end things with him."

The night is not going well. I tell him how I feel, but all he's doing is promising to never sell drugs again and begging me not to leave him. I *have to get out of here.* I go to the bathroom, only to try to speak with his mom. I

tell her I am afraid of him, and I really just want to leave. She helps me get out of the house, and I run to the bus stop, praying for the bus to come before he does. *Thank you, God.*

~ ~ ~

This is bad. Now I'm having nightmares about these people coming in and hurting Mama, as a way get to me, in order to get to Terry. He is calling me off the hook, but I will never again take his call. He calls Mama and cries to her. I hear he is drinking himself to death.

Terry's mom calls and tells Mama that I am killing her son. "Well, I'm not going to let him kill my daughter! I've been a part of that kind of so-called love," Mama says. She doesn't even have the full story. I've never told her that Terry has actually hit me.

All the guys who were up north with Terry are still in jail. He was the only one released. I believe he is being haunted by some kind of guilt.

When I come home after being at a friend's house all day, Terry jumps out of nowhere. *Oh, my God!* "What are you doing here?"

"Who were you with?" He demands to know. Maybe he isn't able to deal with the guilt of what happened up north and having his girlfriend leave him all at the same time.

"A friend."

"A guy friend?" His anger and jealousy issues, coupled with his drinking, make him a time bomb waiting to explode.

"No," I say, while sticking the key into the door. Mama is sitting in the living room. He sees her, turns around, and leaves. I tell Mama that if I come up missing, Terry did it. I believe he is going to kill me one day.

I sleep with a huge bayonet that my friend took from her dad who brought it back from Vietnam. She says I can hold onto it, just in case. I leave my blinds slightly open so I can see anyone approaching. It's horrible. I wake up in the middle of the night, thinking I hear his voice. I am clutching the bayonet, my heart beating fast.

Almost two months pass and things feel okay. I don't hear anything from him. I am still not sleeping without fear, but it is getting easier.

~ ~ ~

It's a new day with the same 10 a.m. yelling wake-up call to her boyfriend. Sounds like Mama's going to bust a blood vessel this time. I'm sure she will need to unwind after all that.

"I'll be back," she says

Yep, running to her good friend Smirnoff…or worse. I try to talk to her about her boyfriend. I am insinuating that she deserves better, and asking how she could deal with all that after dealing with my father. She gets mad, telling me that he is nothing like my father, that he would never hit her, and that he makes her happy.

"You're too young to understand," she says and leaves.

I think I understand very well what it's like to feel like he's all you got, that there is nothing greater out there for you. Mama believes he is better than my father. For her to find out about what he did to Nia, her eldest daughter, would kill her.

At this point, I don't know if my sister and I are enough to keep her alive if he is out of the picture. Most of the crack-addicted mothers I know have let the drug take over every part of themselves, even their appearance. Not Mama. She doesn't have the money to buy the best clothes, but she is always clean, smelling good, and put together. She won't even go outside without lipstick. Can't help but wonder if that's partly due to his presence in her life. She never knows when he will pop over, so she stays ready.

It is 2:00 a.m. and there's no sign of Mama. That's not unusual but it is strange that she hasn't called. I call every friend she has, and no one has seen her. I try one more—an old man she sometimes hangs out with. He tells me yes, she is there at his house, and I should come get her before she O.D.s. He says she's been running around with some guy down the street from him— someone he doesn't trust. He believes he gave her some bad stuff.

At this point in time, I do not own a car. *Who am I going to call to take me to her? I don't have Uncle Tee or Terry to help me.* I go to a neighbor who barely knows me and ask her to take me.

I find Mama laid out on her friend's couch, right where he said she would be. I ask her if she can get up.

"I don't think so," she says. "Everything is spinning."

I lift her body off the couch and take her into the bathroom. I prop her up against the sink and splash water on her face.

"I'm falling, PK."

"No, Mama, I won't let you fall." Mama has experienced things that most of our family would be shocked to hear, but it has not changed her personality. She is still so sweet and naive. When I should be mad at her, my heart aches for her instead.

I've got to get her straightened out enough that I can walk her outside and get her in the car. The neighbor doesn't know about her drug use, but I don't think I can hide it this time. We stumble out the front door. The neighbor's eyes get big. She jumps out of her car and helps me get Mama inside.

"Should we take her to the hospital?"

"No, she'll be fine," I say. I take Mama out of the car and start nursing her. She vomits a few times, but nothing comes out. It is more like dry heaving. She is scared. I ask if I should call 9-1-1. She tells me, "Not yet. Let's see how I feel."

She falls asleep, and I wake her up every thirty minutes until she feels better. That was really scary, even for her. I hope it scares her enough to stop.

~ ~ ~

My heart is pounding. What is happening? *Am I having a heart attack from just walking to the store?* The clerk asks if I'm okay. He can see from my eyes that something is not right. I shake my head no, pay for my things, and leave.

Can I make it home? It's only one block away. I can see my apartment from here, but it feels like I'll never make it there. *Oh, my God, am I dying?* I'm almost there, just a few more feet. As soon as I step into the apartment, it stops. I feel normal. *That was weird.*

It's happening again at my friend's house two doors down. My heart is pounding. I feel as if I might pass out. I go into my friend's kitchen, get a glass of water, and try to calm down. *Come on, what is going on?* After a few minutes in the kitchen, I go back into my friend's room where she and her little brother are playing video games. They are talking crazy to each other about who is better at the game while I'm sitting here believing I am about to die.

I've got to go home. Got to get up now and leave. Now, before I die here on their bedroom floor. "I'll see you guys later," I say, jumping up.

Rushing into the apartment, I can hear my heart beating outside of my chest. I tell Mama, and she tells me to go warm up some milk and drink it. She says it will help. I would if we had milk. But we don't, and I am not about to walk out there to go get some. My heart has stopped pounding anyway.

~ ~ ~

Tonight I've been invited to a party at a friend's house. This is a party I have to attend. A few DJs and some rappers will be there. I'm feeling fine. I've been in the house for a few days and the heart palpitations haven't recurred. Maybe I was just tired and needed this rest.

A lot of people I haven't seen since school are here. Rodney, one of the cutest guys from our school, is the DJ. He's a year older, and has beautiful light brown eyes. All the girls over here are drooling. He calls me over and asks me if I want to get on the mic. He says he is going to pass around the mic and tells me I should grab it.

It's packed in here. There are a lot of rappers from the music scene. The mic is on me.

"*What you get, is the pain I feel… What you see is the pain I feel… Whatcha think? It's the pain I feel… Can't hide it's the pain I feel…*

It's deep, the pain I feel…

Go to sleep with the pain I feel… Wake up to the pain I feel…

Stuck with the pain I feel.

Can't let it go, but why hold on?

I'm holding on, but I need to let it go

But the pain's got hold of my throat

And every time I think I'm good—I choke.

I clean, light candles, and soak—at times I have no hope

Alert every time you spoke

Got mine every time you stroked

But our project left me short of a stroke

Good girl gone bad, you made me do it

Why I fuck them other dudes? You made me do it. My chip is huge—but I ain't gon' drop clues

And in turn they gon' keep dropping money for shoes

And I ain't just about the dough

But every dude gon' pay for the pain I know

They gon' hate me for the lack of the things we do

And crave the same love I crave for you. What you get is the pain I feel...

What you see is the pain I feel... Whatcha think? It's the pain I feel... Stuck with this pain I feel."

I do my thing. This is the first time I do that in front of so many people. They love me, but Rodney says it was just cool, and I need to work on my timing.

After the party, my neighbor Stephanie, her little brother, and I are walking home, and all I can think about is what Rodney said. I take it a little hard. But, okay—my timing.

"Is that Terry's car?" Stephanie asks.

"Oh, my God! Run!" We run to the back of an apartment building and hop over two brick walls to get to our apartment. We run up the stairs and go into my neighbor's house before Terry can see us. We look out the window and see him pull off.

"What am I running for? He don't want me," Stephanie says. "Me either," her brother adds.

No, it's me he wants. "Bye, you guys." Although I see Terry pull off, I can't help but wonder if he's waiting on the steps for me. I walk slowly to my apartment, and then when I get close, I run in. What am I going to do about him?

8

Sixteen Melodies

Mama never does find a good job. She is smart when she applies herself, and can do almost anything, but alcohol has such a strong hold on her. It is the only consistent thing in her life—well, except for me. She works here and there—as a receptionist, on an assembly line building parts for planes, and as a care provider for elderly people. These jobs are all short lived. She relies on public assistance until Nia and I are too old for her to get it anymore. A year ago, she fell and shattered her ankle, and now she's on permanent disability.

We don't see much of Nia anymore. She's off doing her own thing. After she graduated from high school, she became close to the neighbors downstairs. They converted her, and now she's a Jehovah's Witness. She had a letter taped to the side of her dresser that she'd written to

God, telling Him how sorry she was for everything. The neighbors got hold of her at the right time. She was ready to change her life.

As for Terry, I'm not sure whether or not he is still on my trail, but there is a dark cloud following me. It's been with me since I was six. It's not hovering over me or anything, but it wants its presence known. If it could talk, it would say, "Hey! Don't get too happy, I'm right over here."

Bring it on. I have my boxing gloves on and I'm ready. I now know that I am more than the daughter of a pimp or the designated caretaker of a substance abuser. I am no longer that little girl who was hiding behind the closet door and I am not scared. I have a passion I love and it loves me back. It has *become* me. I have found a power in my words that I cannot describe.

Tiny is into the power of words too, and we both want to do hip-hop. She's a girl I know from back in high school. Her grandmother lives in our apartment building. She was two years ahead of me in school, but now I'm twenty-one and she is twenty-three. We meet up again with the intention of forming a rap group. She's light skinned with a little waist and big breasts, and all the boys think she's sexy. I think she looks like Betty Boop.

Since we're trying to do the rap thing, she introduces me to Reign, a rapper she dated when she was sixteen. "He's an okay-looking dude," she says, "but he's real cool. He'll work on the rhyming with us to get us tight."

When I write down my life story and put it to music, it helps me deal with the pain and aggression. *What you get is the pain I feel... What you see is the pain I feel... Whatcha think? It's the pain I feel...*

~ ~ ~

Reign is twenty-two, and he's light brown like me. But he's taller which is rare. I was always the tallest person in my class. We're at his house almost every day, getting tight with our lyrics. While we're working, I often see him checking me out with those sleepy eyes of his. He looks like he smokes marijuana but he doesn't. He's just a real calm spirit.

He is the tightest rapper I've ever heard. He's in a rap duo with Easy. They call themselves Asylum Life. Easy is Reign's best friend, and a real slick dude. He has a roughness about him, but it's subtle—a quiet storm. He's good looking with dark brown skin and bowlegs. He has braces on his teeth, but on him they are kind of sexy.

Reign is better with metaphors and better at telling stories, but Easy raps extremely fast. His mouth is like a machine gun, but you can make out every word he says. Not everyone can do that. They both graduated from Crenshaw High, where they were considered the battle kings. They destroyed everybody they rapped against.

Today could change everything, and I can't get out of the house fast enough. Mama had another night of drinking too much and this morning she is irritable. But I will not let that throw me off course. I have to shake her off, focus, and not let her ruin my moment. Reign and Easy are hooked up with guys who manage musicians and try to take them mainstream. Reign suggests we meet them. I'm excited and nervous to meet managers of musicians.

We're on Clinton Street at a home studio. I'm in a house full of guys I don't know, in a neighborhood with its own notorious reputation. I feel slightly awkward and a little unsafe. But, they have more gear than we're used to and to us novices, it feels like a full-fledged studio. We are getting ready to do our thing, and hoping all of Reign's coaching pays off. There's a microphone stand in the middle of the living room and a keyboard with a small track board off in the corner.

Tiny and I are standing before five rappers and two managers, getting ready to bust rhymes. I always go first. They say my style is reminiscent of MC Lyte, a mainstream rapper from the East Coast. That feels good because East Coast rappers are really doing it big right now. I'm nervous, but I'm taking that nervous energy and making it work for me. I step up and do my thing. Asylum Life's managers tell me my voice is strong and my lyrics are intimidating. I feel good.

Tiny is up next. She has a sweet, small voice, kind of squeaky, and her lyrics are nasty and sexual. They love the combination. One of the managers pulls out a contract, and we are signing on the spot. *Gotcha!* I feel like I did when I was six years old and snared those two birds in the cardboard box.

We are now female rappers, rolling with real managers. The owner of the company is Big Gee, a man well respected on the streets. This is not my neighborhood, so I'm not familiar with him, but I can tell just by the look in his eyes that he doesn't play. You don't go up against this man. The intimidation doesn't come from his face or his stance—it's all in the eyes. I know that look. I've seen it many times, in the eyes of the small-timers on my block. But, this man's look is much bigger, much bolder. He's definitely worked the streets.

We've only known him a short time, but he says something to us that is profound. "You need to write ya' own rhymes. No dude can tell ya' story like you can."

This changes the way I think about writing and I know I'll never forget it. All the female rappers we know have men writing for them, but this advice leads us to pen a song called "School'n Um." It's about teaching dudes a thing or two about how women think or get down. We win showcase after showcase, bringing home first-place trophies and plaques.

~ ~ ~

On Clinton and Ross, I start to feel like a real MC. Hanging and working with Reign and Easy is great preparation, and it's getting us ready for the big leagues. If you can rock with them, you can rock with anyone.

We don't have a record deal yet, but who's really thinking about that? Just being picked up by managers feels big time to us. We're doing what we love, and everyone says we're mad skillful at it.

Mama's always said I was good with words, but I don't want to tell her just yet. I know she'll be happy for me, but I want to keep it to myself for a while. She will want to come and support me, and I'm not sure I'm ready to share this arena with her.

~ ~ ~

Tiny and I are at the studio every day, laying down music. I know if things can remain calm like this just a while longer, we can make it. The cloud over my life isn't hanging as heavy lately. I feel like I'm almost there.

All the fellas go out to eat, so Tiny and I stay at the studio with the engineer, working. If I don't get things just right, I'll do take after take. Tiny gets mad at me sometimes. One time I do so many takes, the engineer leaves us to record ourselves. I am lying on the floor, half asleep, trying to get that damn thing right. As time goes by, this happens less and less. Reign's coaching pays off.

We hear some commotion in the streets. Someone

says Big Gee was just murdered at a restaurant. We know Reign and some of the others are there with him. *What happened? And what about Reign and Easy? Are they hurt?*

The boys are all really upset. You can hear the crying from the street as they make their way to the front door. This is the first time we've ever seen these men show any emotion or vulnerability at all, and it's hard to know what to say to them.

I follow Reign outside to the porch. He's sad and upset but much calmer than the others. I wrap my arms around him and we cry together. The others are still inside, loudly mourning their loss. The silence out here is comforting. We sit like this for a while, not saying a word, and I can feel a bond growing, a connection I shouldn't feel. It's pulling us closer together. *What am I doing? This is Tiny's ex!* I can't stop the feeling, and I can see that he's feeling it too.

In the weeks following Big Gee's passing, Reign and I talk about everything—Terry, the abuse. I tell him that I haven't heard from Terry in some time, but I can't be sure he has completely let me go. "He could still be a potential problem."

Reign is unconcerned with Terry. "If he becomes a problem, I'll handle it." We have a more immediate problem on our hands—Tiny. Reign and I are solidly together now, and the closer we get, the more Tiny adds to the story of her involvement with Reign. It was only a few months ago that she told me she never took their relationship too seriously. "We were young, and I had another man at the time."

Now, when she talks about him, it's more like, "We were in love!"

She doesn't come right out and ask me to reconsider being with Reign, but she puts some serious guilt on me. This goes on for weeks, and every week it seems like she adds another story. The subject of pregnancy makes its way into the mix, but Reign says that's news to him. "Far as I knew, it was puppy love—nothing more."

Reign worries I might change my mind about him but there's no way. At least that's how I feel at the moment. I could use a few days away from the studio to sort out my thoughts and feelings. I take a break from the studio, but breaking from Reign is impossible. *How can I walk away from something so beautiful? From someone who distracts me from home, soothes the ache of poverty, and eases the constant worry that is Mama?*

I am no longer alone, escaping into song. When Reign and I are together, we're a melody.

My mind is made up. I want to be with him. Tiny realizes that we really care about each other, and she drops the subject. Even though she never speaks about it again, the resentment is there in her eyes any time he and I show affection to each other. But my bond with Tiny is too strong for a boy to come between us. We never argue.

We never lay aside our friendship for any reason, even when something comes up that could stop it cold. We get through the crisis and hold it together. It seems fitting our rap duo is called Remedy.

We are surrounded by rap legends. Clinton Street is home to a famous, unsigned, underground group. There's also a big-time rapper on this street. He's a West Coast favorite, who happens to come from Compton—my hometown. It's DJ Quik! How crazy is it that DJ Quik and I came from the same hometown, lived not too far from each other, and ended up on the same street?

Quik's a big star over here. I've been asked to do a song with the lead member of the underground rap group, but I don't meet Quik yet. I watch him from a distance. If he made it, I can make it!

Now that Big Gee is gone, Asylum Life loses the record deal they were signing before he died. It's the final straw for Clinton, and time for us all to do our own thing. Clinton Studio is shut down.

This is not over! I will be in the music business and I will be successful. One way or another, I will get Mama out of the ghetto so she can concentrate on getting her life back. There is too much temptation here. Mama tries, but there is always some drug user or alcohol abuser next door or down the street. And Mama makes friends with every-body, including the local bums and hobos. Most of these mothers who are on drugs are mean, paranoid, and stay away from suspicious-looking people. Not my mama.

I go up to the Laundromat where Mama is washing clothes, and I see a bum sitting there with a can of beer bought for him by Mama.

"Not to worry," she says, "They're cool. They need to be talked to, PK, not just thrown away."

"Yeah, whatever, Mama. It's embarrassing," I say. I walk away, pissed, embarrassed, and disgusted.

They appreciate her so much, but now I have bums for lookouts, and my friends are starting to connect them with me. The bums are always asking me, "You alright? You need anything?" *And if I did, what are you going to do to help me?* I call them the Bum Squad.

~ ~ ~

Asylum Life will always be my rap crew, but I soon link up with Taylor, an old friend from Compton whose father manages acts. Taylor is an incredible rapper, and the one who gave me my first kiss in my garage when I was ten years old. When he gets word that I am rapping in L.A., he gets my number and reaches out to me. After we catch up, he asks me to send him and his father some music. They listen to the three songs I send them, and invite me to meet at their office.

Here they are after all this time! I sit in a conference room with them, still a little shy with Taylor over that kiss. He was my first crush.

They love my songs, my voice, and my delivery. They compare me to MC Lyte, and then call in Janice Banter. She is wearing the shortest white shorts I've ever seen. They show off her voluptuous body. She is the boss over here and the wife of an infamous crime figure. She's running this business for him while he's in prison, serving a sentence of thirty years for extortion and God knows what else. I've never met him, but I've heard stories. I don't know what this means to me. I just want to do music.

I'm now a solo act with a new manager and a deal with a production company. Tiny and I still hook up and do shows here and there around town, and I'm still holding down Asylum Life. But I'm hanging with a new rap crew.

~ ~ ~

I really want to take the plunge and move into a place of my own without Mama, but I worry that she can't make it without me. Tiny and I decide to go ahead and get an apartment with her childhood friend Alexandra—Alex for short.

We find a townhouse on Crenshaw, one of the most famous streets in Los Angeles. This is no Rodeo Drive in Beverly Hills. It's the 'hood all the way. On Sunday nights, the streets fill up with beautiful cars with hydraulics that the drivers use to make the cars bounce, showing off their skills. The women try to look their best to catch all the guys with money, the 'hood's rich guys, the ballers who own those beautiful classic cars with murals and graphics.

Meanwhile, this label deal is causing me too much stress. First of all, I feel like I'm paying the price for the shadow cast by Janice's notorious husband. Janice is an artist in her own right, but she is having problems getting respect in that area. She is being blackballed because of her husband's history. Now *I'm* being blackballed.

Not only that, but the label is not delivering on their promises. I am only getting minimal recording time, and they have been unable to lock down distribution—which they told me was already in place when they signed me. It's going to take some doing, but I have to get off this label.

I confront Janice about not delivering on what was promised to me as an artist on their label. But she refuses to let me out of my contract. They're holding on tight. She tries to entice me with the single she did with this old-school group. I write a rap verse for the song with them and perform it on the video. I get paid to do it, and the money comes in handy, but I'm still not content. I want out.

After the recording, Janice passes me her cell phone. It's the big boss on the other end, calling from prison. I've heard all these stories about him being notorious for many things. Hearing his voice come through the phone line is unnerving. *Uh-oh, what if he knows I want to leave the label? What is he going to do—or have done—to me?*

The conversation is surprisingly peaceful. He tells me that he understands my concerns, and asks me to give them four more months to make it happen. If it doesn't work by then, I can go. I agree and get back to work, anticipating my album release.

The four-month window opens and shuts and still no album release. But ending the agreement proves tougher than the big boss made it sound like it would be. Janice fights me on it, and there is an implied threat behind her words. Even though they're not standing behind what they told me in terms of getting things happening for me in four months or letting me go, a deal is a deal. I'm leaving one way or another. I'm out. Now I'd better watch my back.

~ ~ ~

The money I get from doing the verse for Janice's song covers my part of the move-in costs, but now Alex cannot come up with her part. I am eager to move in and take full ownership of my independence, so I come up with a plan. I go back to a hustler from my old neighborhood and convince him to give me a few sacks of dope to sell here in L.A. *Wow! Now what am I going to do?*

I go and talk to Shadow from the Bum Squad. I call him Shadow for two reasons—the dirt, and the fact that he's as black as a shadow. He's lived in this neighborhood his whole life. He knows who's who and what's what. He puts the word out to a few base heads. "No women," I tell him. In two days, I'm all out of dope and going back to get more. Then I go back again and again. Shadow tells Mama. I am completely ashamed.

I feel like a hypocrite—all these years begging Mama to stop using and now I'm involved with the stuff myself. I realize I lost myself for a minute. I give Shadow some money and buy him a few t-shirts (black, of course, not white), socks, and a pair of boots.

Then I pay to move us into the apartment, and swear never to touch the stuff again. I keep my word—but that doesn't mean we don't know how to have a good time. We party, and when I say party, that's an understatement. I know the landlord is sorry he let us in here. Every night we have it cracking loudly. We even have the neighbors over who live across the courtyard from us. The court-yard is where it really goes down. No respect is given to the surrounding neighbors. It's terrible.

Tiny is feminine—but she thinks like a boy. I never hear her mention the word love. I never see her kiss a guy or hold hands. Yet there are about three boys at our house party right now that she's been with. She picks them just for satisfaction—but not like a whore. They have an understanding, and it is what it is. There's never any drama. They love her like a good friend and they are always there for her. She has some kind of spell on them.

Alex is also known as Mack. She got that name in high school for being a heart breaker. (Where I come from, a Mack is someone who has a lot of women; she's a female Mack.) She's a very beautiful girl—half Spanish, half Black. We have a bit more in common as it relates to men.

Like me, she loves them. It's not just about pleasure. But unlike me, as soon as she's done, she's done. She doesn't feel she needs to explain herself. She's a heart breaker. I can't tell you how many phone calls we have to take just to give her sobbing victims someone to talk to.

Reign is not feeling my girls and how hard they party. I'm here and I'm with it, but I can never party as hard as Tiny and Alex. I'm in a relationship so I have to be careful how far I go. There is no question that we have the liveliest apartment on the Shaw. (We call Crenshaw "the Shaw" for short.) There are liquor bottles lined up, and domino and spades tables set up. Sometimes, when I come home from Reign's house, we can't get in the apartment without having to step over dudes still drunk from the night before.

Reign gets disgusted and demands that I stay in my room. He is afraid to leave me here. He worries I might succumb to temptation and cheat, but he doesn't have to worry about me. My mind is only on one thing—the bigger picture. His skill set is what I need in my life to keep me tight with my craft.

No amount of temptation is going to make me slip up and sleep with any of these guys in here. Trust me. They try. They get mad because they can't have it. They look at Reign sideways, wondering what he has that they don't. Most of them have more money. Maybe they even have the looks on him. But there is a greater energy guiding me.

I can see the big picture so clearly. Most of the guys I come across serve no purpose for the big picture, while others do. More often than not, there is a price to be paid. In order to be with a guy who meets my needs in the ways that are most important to me, I have to sacrifice other needs.

I agree to stay at Reign's house the majority of the time to keep him secure. When I come home, I have dudes I don't even know calling me "Oklahoma." I'm not sure how they decide on that nickname, but that is their way of saying I am always away. Reign cannot take it anymore. We're moving into our own apartment in Inglewood.

~ ~ ~

Things couldn't be better—well, besides me being a little lonely. Reign now works a nine-to-five job, doing construction. After Clinton shuts down, he goes to work with his older brother. He works long hours, and when he comes home, he's dirty and tired, and most of the time, he just falls asleep. We don't argue or anything but he's antisocial and I'm a social butterfly. We don't go anywhere together. I'm always at the studio, and he is either at home or at work. I swear we haven't made love in over a month. I really love him, and I want to show him how much I appreciate him taking care of the household bills and supporting my quest to be an artist.

Mama is unable to sustain her apartment. The disability check helps, but it's not enough. After being late on the rent, or missing it altogether several times, she gets evicted. Now she is moving in with Reign and me. This is just a small, one-bedroom apartment, with barely enough room for the two of us.

She completely takes over the living room, but it's easier than having her in her own apartment. At least now she's not calling me, drunk and out of her mind, and making it impossible for me to sleep because I am so worried about her dying on me. And this is better than running over to her apartment every time she doesn't answer her phone for an hour.

None of my friends know about Mama's drug use. Tiny sees her drunk once or twice, but that's all. It's not just the drinking that embarrasses me. Mama is very clean and put together but she still wears clothes from the old days. And she's eccentric. She travels with plastic bags of clothes instead of a suitcase. Now she is cutting polyester pants to make shorts.

Mama is drunk. *How can I hide this from Reign?* I can't. I have to trust him with this information and hope he doesn't hold it against me.

He doesn't. In fact, he doesn't see what the big deal is. Most people don't. Mama is fun and loving when she's drinking, and I'm usually accused of being too hard on her. No one understands. I only have my music to escape into. I grab my notepad and earphones and leave them both in the living room.

~ ~ ~

For several years, I deal with Mama's issues, but give most of my time and energy to my music. I work with extremely successful producers, including one who is also signed to Janice's label. He is to them what Dr. Dre is to Death Row Records. In fact, Janice's label has a connection to Death Row Records. But I just want to do music, so I do my best to stay out of that drama. And believe me, it is big drama. I feel like I could get hit by a stray bullet at any time.

We're all here at the studio working. Most of us are in the common area, watching TV. My heart is pounding and I feel like I am going to black out. This hasn't happened to me in years. *I've got to get up and walk to the door for some air. Oh, no, it's not working. This is it.* I get Reign on the phone. "Please come get me. I think I'm having a heart attack."

He's on his way. "Tell someone there to help you 'til I get there!" But I don't. I just stand at the front door, breathing the fresh air until he gets here. "You okay?" he says.

"No, just take me home, please."

Several days pass, and I leave the house only once, and get stuck in the middle of the freeway. I am paralyzed with fear and unable to move. Someone calls the police to get me off the freeway. I don't leave the house again after that. The only way I can leave is if Reign is with me.

Mama says it seems like I'm having panic attacks. *Panic attacks? Most of the time when it happens, I'm sitting in a relaxed environment, doing nothing.*

A few days later, Reign comes home with a book: *Understanding and Controlling Panic Attacks.*

~ ~ ~

I'm not interested in reading this book. I just need to get up and go outside...force myself to do it...open the door...take a deep breath. *One-two-three-go!* I feel my heart start to pound. I don't even make it down two steps. Oh, please don't do this to me. *After all I've been through in my life, now I can't leave the house?*

I pick up the book. It instructs me to visualize what I've done as if I've already done it. Visualize walking into the grocery store, for example. Visualize myself putting my things in the basket, pushing the basket to the cash register, paying for my groceries, walking out to the parking lot, putting everything in my car, and driving home without incident. Then go and do it exactly that way. I suspect this may be easier said than done but it's worth a shot. I start incorporating these visualization techniques into my life.

It is time for me to get back into the studio. This will be the real test. *Will visualization really help me?* Reign wants to go with me, just in case. But I can't test the technique unless I'm by myself. I visualize it all—the route I will take, getting there, recording, having fun, and laughing. So now I really do it.

It works! It gets me here. Now that I'm here with everyone, I'm feeling a little panicked. I go into the bathroom and apply the happy-place technique, where I visualize a place where I feel safe. I see myself lying beside a creek with the sun shining down on me at just the right temperature. A colorful leaf is being carried downstream. I follow that leaf, keeping my eye on it until the panic subsides.

The panic stops long enough for me to record this song. Now I will have to do visualization all over again to get myself back home. Mama and Reign worry about me until I make it home. It is challenging, but I make it. I will continue to do visualization until I beat this thing. The panic-attack book also says to avoid stressful situations. I know that I have been under a lot of stress in my life. Terry hasn't been a factor for a long while, but I can't avoid the stress that comes from worrying about Mama.

9

Through the Broken Glass

The music business is proving very difficult to navigate. It's not just me— it's all women. We are not taken seriously. Many women compromise their bodies and integrity to get in. I will not be a whore, and I will not be pimped for music. But this is my only way out of the life I was born into. It is my only way to turn the life I have into the life of my dreams, in which there is no poverty and Mama is healthy.

I'm not going to let anything tear me away from my music, but I don't see how I'm supposed to go up against Janice. When Taylor and his father decided to leave the label, it did not go over well at all. I've already had several calls from the muscle that represents the label, letting me know they are not going to stand for that kind of disrespect. How is it disrespectful to want what was promised or to want out of a negative situation? The label is mostly angry with Taylor's dad, who they feel is doing shady business behind their back.

Anyway, Taylor is at my apartment tonight, telling me about the latest drama. Mama and Reign do not want me to go outside to speak with him, but I tell him to pull into the driveway. I get into his car with him so we can talk. As he is telling me the whole story, I can't believe how dangerous and out of control everything has become. The label is threatening his father's life, and Taylor doesn't feel safe at home.

As we are talking, I notice something strange. A van drives by at a very slow speed, and when it's a few yards from us, a teenage kid of maybe fifteen or sixteen drops out the side door and starts walking down the street. The van continues in the same direction the kid is walking, so why drop the kid outside the van?

That's strange. Taylor continues to talk, unaware of what I'm watching go down.

Meanwhile, a man in an Adidas sweat suit and white gloves is walking toward the boy. This is also strange. They pass each other, and when he gets just past Taylor's car, he stops.

"Go Taylor! Go! Drive!" I shout.

He doesn't see what I see, so he doesn't know why I'm shouting for him to go. But he's already nervous about what's going on with the label. So, he puts the car in reverse, backs out, flips it into drive, and drives as fast as he can—in the same direction as the van. He is oblivious to the fact that he's driving straight into the middle of the danger. When I tell him what I witnessed and let him know he's going straight for them, he reaches behind the seat and pulls out a gun. And then he punches the gas, trying to pass the van.

Right as we are about to pass the van, we see the boy duck down and take off running into the mortuary parking lot. This tells me I am right—something is about to go down and he's a part of it. We hit the corner so fast that the van that was carrying the boy hits the corner behind us.

The police pull us over. *Thank God!* They say they pulled us over because we hit the corner so fast that a bus almost sideswiped us. Taylor tells them what happened and explains that we were afraid for our lives. They let us go without checking the car. Someone is watching over us.

He drops me off. I am stunned. I can't believe he had that gun. Taylor is like me. We stay out of trouble. That was a close call. Something really bad was about to go down. I am certain that if the police hadn't happened to show up, whoever was in the van would have started shooting up Taylor's car. Thankfully, Mama and Reign are none the wiser.

Within a few days, I learn more about what went on. Taylor and I were sitting in his father's car—a car with tinted windows, which made it difficult to see who was inside. Whoever was in the van thought it was Taylor's father sitting in the car, and at the last minute realized they were wrong. We were nearly victims of mistaken identity.

Without any explanation, I am suddenly let off the label. The only thing I can figure is that Janice realizes that enough is enough, and decides to let me go.

That experience changes my love for the music business. I don't see it the same way anymore. I have to figure out how to make it work for me. I'm living with some harsh realities, and I have to think like a businesswoman. In fact, I have to think like a man. I'm no longer in it just for the love. I'm also in it for the money.

~ ~ ~

Oh, great…another hustler who thinks he knows how to run a label. This time the problem is that the label has four acts, and one studio, and one of the acts is hogging all the studio time. It has been over a year since I was signed to the label, and I only have five good songs. Chance, the star act on the label, has been with them less than half the time I have, but they have a whole album.

Time is running out and it feels like a matter of life and death. I realize I have to say my goodbyes to another label. I am finally free of anxiety and panic attacks, and I will not willingly continue to place myself under the kind of heavy stress that triggers those attacks. I've heard too many stories about people imprisoned in their own homes by anxiety. I will not let myself regress.

I form an alliance with David, the lead singer of Chance. He is twenty-four-years old and about five-foot-ten-inches tall. He's a little short for me, given that I'm five-foot-seven barefoot and five-foot-nine in heels. His smooth chocolate skin and athletic physique make up for his stature.

David has the body of an NFL running back, with his muscular, strong legs and wide shoulders. He lives in basketball shorts and sleeveless shirts, ready to play ball at any time. He says he knows the NBA could pick him up, but he'd rather sing. He's totally cocky and somewhat conceited, but I think it's cute. The fact that he reminds me of my father in every way, from the shape of his hands to the tone of his skin, tells me I need to be running as fast as I can. But I'm so intrigued by him.

~ ~ ~

I'm a hip-hop artist, but I have a real flair for love songs. I've written a few, but no one is really trying to hear a rapper say she has R&B songs. David gives me a shot. We start writing songs together, and we're told we have a really romantic sound.

Reign and I have been together for about four years, but for the past year I've been having a secret love affair in my head with David. I'm coming home late and spending most of my time with David. Reign knows we are on the same label and write songs together, and he suspects there might be something else going on. But what can he really say? David and I are working.

I'm completely and undeniably in love with David. I've never felt this before, not with Terry and not with Reign. The unexpected kiss in the studio while working late one night doesn't help. We are working late, sitting at the console talking, and I can feel the energy that's been building between us all day. When he leans in for a kiss, I don't stop it.

I have been looking in all the wrong places for the right man, and letting despair drive my choices. But David comes into my life out of nowhere. I wasn't looking for him. Now we'll just have to see if he's going to be the best thing that ever happens to me or my downfall.

~ ~ ~

In my sleep this morning, I mistakenly call Reign David. I try to play it off but it's not working. Reign is leaving me. He asked me to marry him on Christmas morning, but he takes the ring back today, a little more than a month later. I hate for us to end this way.

I am overwhelmed with guilt over hurting him and ruining the place where Mama and I can be together under the same roof. So I beg, with a closed bathroom door between us, for him to give me a second chance. He refuses. He has been good to me. We just grew apart.

I feel like David is the one for me, and I have to be with him. He's someone I will be able to love my entire life. Before Mama and I walk out of the house to move in with David, Reign says something that I hope is not true. "You will never be happy with any man." He says I'm looking for a father— something I'll never find in a romantic relationship with any man. Then he tells me I have abandonment issues, and I am becoming my father.

Reign knows this will hurt me, and it does. I trusted him with my feelings about my father's absence. He throws them in my face to ease his own pain. I don't know what is wrong with me or what I'm looking for. I just know this is not it. Sorry, Reign.

He thinks I'm ready for the platinum eight carats in weight
But more ready for the platinum times five in DJ crates...
I'm high stakes...

Blind when it comes to love and mine when it comes to dubs

I grind when it comes to rhymes and on time for the show
I'm for the shine.

It's masturbation receiving crowd participation

Young sperms, they sweat what I makes,

Cause other chicks are square cakes, all talk and no papes

Now you secretly studying my chiseled face... you wanna taste? Fantasizing you're on my waist... impressed by my weight.

I'm a bombshell, and you unimpressed by your date

'cause I'm steak and she oatmeal eel...

The money's to blame, and I'ma do the same thing

Push fat cars, leaving scars on them cats who ain't content with who dey are

Get ya shit, roll ya whips, lace ya wrist, rock ya hips, lick ya lips, perk ya tits

This is for chicks who are living splendid

And ain't settling down till the fun has ended...

~ ~ ~

David is now my air. We do everything together. We've become PK and David. You cannot mention him without me or me without him. We are an unbreakable pair. We're even starting to look alike—or he's starting to look more like me, anyway. We literally sleep on top of each other, like one body. We could be poor and living in a cardboard box, and I would still love him. You cannot break us apart. We even pee on the toilet at the same time. He sits. I then sit on top of him and pee between his legs.

"Spit in my mouth," he says while making love to me. "I want to be closer to you. I want to be part of you."

How can we literally become one? I pierce our fingers with a needle and mix our blood. I did that with my best friend when I was younger, and we are still friends. It's childish, I know, but it's all I have to guarantee it. Our hearts beat as one. We laugh uncontrollably. Neither of us has ever felt this before.

I'm not uncomfortable the way I usually am when I talk to him about my past or about Mama. He embraces us both with knowing about our rotten life. He ends things with his three-year-old son's mother back in his hometown, and after only a year of dating, he proposes.

I have twenty-five thousand dollars saved from a few of my guest-star appearances. David and I use the money to get a car and pay a few months in advance on our apartment in Studio City. We start to plan our wedding. I ask Mama's brother, Uncle Cook, to give me away since my father has always been erratic and undeserving. But at the last minute, I reach out to my father. Surprisingly enough, he answers the phone and accepts.

After four months of planning, it's my big day. I should be worried that my father won't show up. One time when I was younger, he told me to pack my bags to go to Louisiana for a summer with the whole family. Mama spent the little money she had buying me summer clothes and packing them in a shiny, new, small, red suit-case. I sat on the porch, waiting for hours for him to pick me up, but he never showed.

He's here now, and I'm glad he's standing beside me. I am also experiencing an unbelievable array of other feelings. I thought I'd be filled with joy and be giddy with happiness, but instead I'm being hammered by guilt and shame. My father and I are standing behind the double doors that lead into the church. I hear the song start to play, telling me that the doors will open any minute to reveal my soon-to-be husband, and all eyes will be on me.

I'm so nervous, I think I'm going to be sick. *Lord, please do not let me throw up.*

"You know, BK, we can just leave right now. This is your last chance to get away," my father says.

I turn and look at him, and all the guilt and shame flash before me. *This should not be you. It should be Uncle Cook.* At the last minute, I told my uncle that he would not be the one to give me away; I was choosing the man who

has never been here for me over him.

I glance toward the street. What if Reign walks through the church door and stops the wedding because I broke his heart? I feel short of breath. *Oh, no…not now. Please hurry up and get me to this altar.* The doors open, and David is standing there looking so handsome that tears begin to fall from my eyes.

My father is giving me away to my soon-to-be husband, but every time I look at David's face, more guilt hits me.

I don't deserve this happiness. *It's your fault, Daddy. It's your fault that I was in what most people would call a sick relationship with Uncle Tee. Where were you? And how on earth can I marry David without telling him about that time in my life? How can I ever really be his princess?*

No, it was all me. I made some bad decisions. *God, please bless me with this man. I promise to tell him everything.* But it's my deepest, darkest secret. I've hidden it from the world, and it needs to stay hidden because no one will understand it.

I hold it together and get through the ceremony. "I now pronounce you man and wife," the preacher says. "Introducing the Allens!"

It's done. I'm in my mid-twenties, and

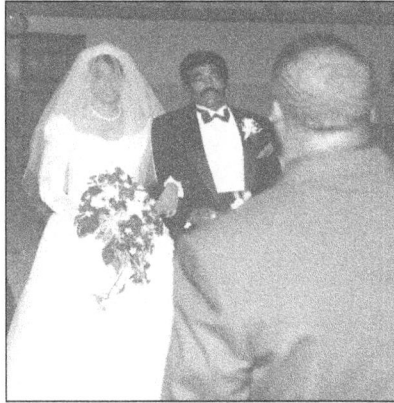

Wedding Day

married to the man of my dreams. I couldn't be happier. I deserve this. My head says it, so why am I still seeing that dark cloud?

His eighteen-year-old brother—the best man—moves in with us right after the I do's. I met David's three-year-old son at the wedding rehearsal, and he called me Mom and blew a kiss at me. This is all overwhelmingly beautiful. I am now a woman with my own family to look after.

~ ~ ~

Most of our money goes into the wedding, but I get ten thousand dollars from a production company to look over some contracts and set up a few things for its label. I've never set up a label before, but I've been signed to enough bad ones to know what not to do. This puts me ahead of the game.

David is not himself anymore. He tries and fails to break down one music industry door after another, and this sends him into a tailspin of depression. He's taking me with him. *Why can't things ever stay good for me?* I swear it feels like I've been fighting to get by ever since birth.

I'm working on a few projects, including my first solo album, Introducing Peeps Game. This title comes from something a street rapper says to me. I look up to this guy, and one day, he says, "I like you, little mama. You just sit back and peep game when all these other broads are yapping. Keep it up, and you'll be a boss." He's got that right. I'm an observer in the streets, in the studio, and in life. I watch without speaking, soaking up as much game as possible to get ahead. *Ladies and gentlemen, Introducing Peeps Game.*

~ ~ ~

I partner up with some Canadians who own a studio, and the studio becomes home to me. Now that I'm unsigned, I'm recording more than I did when I was with a label. I work on my recordings with Tiny, who is still doing her usual partying. She can really go hard for being so small. Nobody can drink her under the table. I have personally seen this little mama put big dudes on their backs to the point where she has to take them home. Where does she put it all?

We enlist another member, who is from Inglewood and ill on the mic. She's about five-feet-seven-inches tall, and they call her Slim because she's so skinny. I have seen her take the thoughts right out of a competitor's head; she's that good. We are now known as the rap trio Nsomnia Kafe.

~ ~ ~

I'm working late in the studio when they announce over the intercom that I have a phone call. I immediately think it must be Mama with an emergency. We always keep the decibel level at a hundred, so I take the phone into the hallway. It doesn't help; I can still hear the bass rumbling through the walls.

"Hello," I say.

"Is this Peeps Game?"

"Yeah, who's this?"

"Baby girl, this is DJ Quik. I just had to call and let you know my manager has been bumping your album in the car all weekend, and I think you're incredible. I want to meet you."

"When?"

"Right now."

DJ Quick is on his way. We shut down the back studio. I light candles and set the mood for my vibe.

He walks in wearing a white t-shirt, black jeans, and French braids all going back on his head. He's about five-feet-ten-inches tall, brown, and thin but in shape.

"I wanted to shake the hand of the girl who was rhyming like that," he says.

I cue the music, wondering if I should tell him that we come from the same hometown, and even lived on the same street many years later. I decide not to. I never really tell anyone I'm from Compton. I love my city, but it gets a bad rap. To avoid judgment, I keep it to myself and just represent Los Angeles—South Central, if you will. It's a Catch-22 for my rap career. Hailing from Compton can be a plus. Some of the most popular and most successful rappers call Compton home, including DJ Quik, Yoyo, NWA, and Compton's Most Wanted.

"I'll have my manager get in touch with you," he says, after listening to some tracks.

We take pictures to capture this important moment in my life and music career, and he leaves.

~ ~ ~

After a few days, his manager calls, saying he already

has a record deal set up for me. The record label houses many famous rappers from both the East and West Coast. Quik's manager takes me over to Loud Records, and the owner puts together the deal and signs me. My life is getting ready to change. I'm ready to get my shot. I can buy a house with a guesthouse in back. I can finally help Mama get on track.

After I have that meeting and receive my advance money, Quik's manager sticks a contract in my face, letting me know that either I sign with him or the deal's off. The manager's company would be my mother company and they would deal with Loud on my behalf.

No way. I go to Loud, tell them I can't take their deal, and let them know the reason why. When they hear this, they let me know they want me anyway. They tell me to stick with them and forget about signing with the managers. I know better. The managers feel responsible for making the deal happen—and they're right. I can't go against them.

Since I cannot accept the deal, I have to give back the advance money. It is just my luck. Once again I am reminded that this is a rotten business. As soon as I dip my toes in the water, the sharks start circling, ready to bite them off.

Mama asks me all the time why I keep trying. Maybe I should do something else. "It's too much heartache," she says.

"What am I going to do? All that keeps me going is the passion for the music and the thought of giving us a better life," I tell her.

~ ~ ~

A brother who is trying to break into the music business after getting out of the drug game introduces me to this rich white man from Spokane, Washington. This brother is one of the smart ones. He joins country clubs and shit, positioning himself around wealthy white people, with none of them wise to his street affiliation.

Mr. Spokane is tall and tanned, with sandy brown hair and the whitest teeth I've ever seen. He's sort of attractive in a straight-laced kind of way. He wears nothing but polo shirts, and he always looks like he's on his way to play golf. In fact, he brags about playing golf with Tiger Woods. Spokane has lots of money and he wants me to sign a recording contract. He is talking big cash for my signature.

Into the studio walk four white men in leather cowboy boots and cowboy hats. They sit there, listening to my street-driving shit. I look around at the country music lovers. *Is there any way in hell they're going to understand this?*

But after Mr. Spokane's daddy and all his friends' leave, Spokane extends his hand. "It's official. I want to sign you now."

I tell him I have a deal on the table with Loud, and

they've already given me a twenty-five thousand dollar advance to sign the deal memo. I tell him there's only one way out of the deal: I would need a non-recoupable fifty thousand dollar advance, and double Loud's recording budget. I don't mention that I've already decided not to go through with the deal with Loud.

"It's a deal!" he says.

What does this guy know about rap music? And, with the kind of money he's sitting on, why is he down in the 'hood recruiting? Is he bored with all the golfing and sky-diving? I can't be concerned with that. There are white folks who can't understand a word we are saying, or don't try to. But they know that rap is big business and they're trying to get a piece of that pie. Congratulations to me.

Although I would love to be with Loud Records and possibly share the stage with some great label mates, leaving isn't so bad when I know I have Mr. Spokane in my back pocket. David agrees that this is a better road to take.

~ ~ ~

Mr. Spokane is talking big shit. He hands me a fifty-thousand-dollar check and puts in an order for a Mercedes-Benz E-class for me, the same color as his. We're getting promo product done up to promote the album, which is coming out soon.

I record at Platinum Studios for a month. Now it's time to give them the first installment payment for my studio time. But I've only heard from Mr. Spokane twice this month. Each time we talk, he promises payment "Tomorrow, tomorrow." Today, I can't get him on the phone, and I'm way past freaking out. It's been at least two weeks since I've heard from him.

I find out he's in jail for fraud, and I'm told he and his family appeared in a news article about their deceptive scams. Independent production companies think that if they know how to make money in the street, or even on Wall Street, then they can do this music shit.

I always try to live my dreams and forget bad memories from my childhood. But the fact is, I am my father's daughter. I have it in me to be a wildcat. Every time something like this happens, it pulls me closer to being ruthless. Almost every day, I have to make a conscious decision to not let my environment dictate my fate.

Just before I signed with Mr. Spokane, I turned this signing shit into a hustle. I went to my attorney and told him that only street hustlers were feeling my music—but they couldn't get the job done. Anybody who wanted to sign me, who hadn't been in the business long enough to know what the hell they were doing, would have to give me non-recoupable advances. I was tired of these people wasting my time. In addition, they would have to release one of my records within a year, or I was automatically out of the contract and could keep my masters.

My attorney is a big time, Jewish man who has a lot of successful artists as clients. "They'll never go for that," he says.

"If they get my music out there, then cool, we're in business. But if they can't pull it off, I keep the loot and the masters, and I'm out of the contract." I decide that is how the game will be played, or I am not playing.

The bad news? Mr. Spokane is in Club Fed somewhere, wearing an orange jumpsuit. That means that once again, I am out of a deal and that damn black cloud is still hovering over my life. I can't seem to hang onto those moments of brightness. As soon as there is a glimpse of light, it gets smothered.

The good news? I have my masters and the loot. I do this for a total of four more deals. Each deal pays fifty thousand dollars, and leaves my masters with me. I stack two hundred thousand dollars doing this. I have the money and maybe this is my cue to become independent, to start my own company.

As for Platinum Studios, I never pay them but we do become great friends. We even go into business together.

~ ~ ~

David and I are still pushing forward with songwriting. We write two songs we feel are perfect for a multi-platinum selling group that is looking for material for their new album. After we wait at Westlake Studios all day, waiting our turn to play our music, the group's manager announces that they've heard all they care to hear. We don't get to play our songs.

We drive home feeling disappointed and shut out. David is talented, but he's also brimming with false pride, and feels everyone should beg to be in his presence. He's a great guy, but he never humbles himself. He's having a string of bad luck.

I get it. My luck hasn't been that great either. I keep climbing the ladder and getting close to the top, and then a moment before reaching it, something knocks me back down to the bottom. Sure, I have a few dollars now, and that has done my family a world of good. But I've wanted to be a rock star since I was six and that craving has only intensified, despite the drama of the music business.

During the ride home, I try to persuade David to go back. We pull into our driveway, and finally I prevail.

"Okay," he says. "But I want you to stay home." David is a hell of a writer, producer, and arranger, who can sound like anybody he wants to, but I am just as much a part of these songs as he is.

I refuse. "I'm just as much a part of this as you. No way in hell am I staying here!"

Back at Westlake, we try to come up with a plan to get ourselves into the studio where they're listening to everybody's music. Their manager comes out, on his way to the kitchen, and spots us.

"Aren't you Devin's friend?" he asks David. Devin is a good friend of David's, who is trying to manage David's career.

Once the guy realizes that David and Devin are friends, he says, "Come in."

I'm nervous, walking though the heavy, triple-thick studio door. Liquor bottles and sushi are everywhere. They turn and look at us. We're standing before maybe nine people, and we're totally on the spot. I sense David's nervousness as he hands the engineer the CD. The engineer gives us a superior look, as though he's judging us already. He's not even part of the damn group.

David tells him to play the songs in a certain order to really get them going. Even though David and I have written a couple of songs together, he's not yet completely confident in my songwriting skills. He has been writing songs since he was ten years old, and so far, I've only written rap and a few R&B songs. So, he wants the songs he had most influence over played first.

The third and final song blares over the large speakers mounted on both sides of the wall. "Hello, millionaires," they say as Jojo, the oldest of the two, reaches out to shake our hands. We're so happy and excited, we can hardly keep it together as we leave the building. We can't celebrate yet, though. We know they have cameras in that room that allow them to look out over the parking lot. So we stay cool.

"Oh, my God!" we scream as we turn the corner. "They want to do both songs!" We're in utter disbelief.

This is the exciting beginning of our songwriting career. Although I'm an MC and David's been writing songs his whole life with his talented group members, his first placement is with me, his wife—an MC from Compton.

~ ~ ~

We work on every album they put out from that point on. We get some gold and platinum plaques and a whole lot of checks. We sign a publishing deal with Warner Chappell for a quarter of a million dollars. Each of us has a fifty-percent share in every song we write and produce—sometimes even more.

We're doing great financially. I launch my own production company to sign and release my own artists. We buy a beautiful home from a famous singer. It sits on top of a hill in Lake Hills, about sixty miles outside of L.A. We can see the lake from our sunken bathtub. We have a two story, four-bedroom home, a dog, and two brand-new cars in the driveway. We have arrived. We can only go up from here.

10

The Blackest Rose

Life is good. We have not gotten any more songs placed over the past three years, but I can't complain. Mama is much better now that she's out here on top of this hill. But every now and again, she gets cabin fever. She takes the metro to L.A. and falls back into the same old trap.

As I sit here in my sunken bathtub with my glass of red wine and the stars shining bright in the sky, Compton becomes a blur. There was an existence before this, but was that a life? No, that was not living. I felt I was holding my breath the entire time. I'm learning to exhale. I wish David could feel the way I am feeling. He has his moments, but his quest to be an R&B singer is a heavy weight on him.

I know why I want it so bad, but I haven't figured out what drives him. I can understand being a creative soul and wanting to excel in your endeavors. But there are times when he becomes extremely bitter about it. My life has had some rotten patches, and his life for the most part has been very good. He grew up with both parents, who love him, and he has a beautiful little son who idolizes him. To my way of thinking, he should be more grateful.

~ ~ ~

Help me! Help me! I wake from yet another nightmare. They have been going since childhood, but they grow increasingly more graphic and horrifying. The dream used to be about me being shot in the stomach while on my way to find Mama somewhere in the street where I could not get to her. My nightmares are still about Mama, but unlike the sketchy, out-of-sequence, hard-to-remember dreams I used to have, these are full-blown horror films. If I do not sit up in bed and write them down, I cannot get back to sleep. Tonight is no different. It's horrible.

I dream that I'm looking for Mama throughout the neighborhood, which becomes desolate and abandoned. I'm close to her. I can feel her. I know she needs me. A man comes up and asks me if I am looking for a woman.

"Yes," I reply.

He tells me that she's at the house of this notorious, terrible man we all know. I race to that house to find the door open. The house looks more like a grey wood shack.

It is completely destroyed. I'm tearing through the place, trying to get to her. She is naked in the bathtub, but there is no water in it. It's Mama except her hair is different, and she has the body she had in her twenties. She is barely able to get up. I throw her arm around my neck and help her out the door.

"Hurry up, PK," she says frantically.

I'm looking back because I figure the terrible man must be coming, but no one is there. She is becoming harder to carry. "Hurry! Hurry!"

"I'm trying, Mama! He's not coming, He is not back there." At this time, she brings my attention to the area under her breast where she has been stabbed twice.

"Oh, my God! Help me. I can't hold her up!" I can't get her to the hospital. I can feel her body getting even heavier. She is dying. I scream, "Help me! Help me!" But there is no one around.

I'm not sure why I have such horrible nightmares. It's ironic, but they seem to come at those times when the horrors of real life subside for a while. When I tell Mama about my nightmares, all she can do is throw her arms around me. My old pal, the dark cloud, never fails to find me.

~ ~ ~

David and I are living off the money from our residuals, which is slowing to a dribble.

I am at my accountant's office, preparing for my label that I am determined to launch. I've been in the studio several times to complete various projects, but what I really want to do is to put Maze's record out. Maze is an actor and a longtime friend of mine. We met at church, around the time I was working on the Loud records deal. We both had albums that were slated to come out at the same time but didn't. He was signed to Atlantic Records at the time.

Later, when all the record companies passed on signing him, I made my decision to use some of my savings to do Maze's project. Now he's my artist, and I will put my all into bringing him a big win. He has some real TV success, but I want to release his first album and create major TV roles for him. I really believe in him and his project.

David's plans aren't going very well. He is trying to stay positive, but it has been a while since our last song placement. This means our writing career is more than slowing to a crawl.

~ ~ ~

I am fighting to get my label up and running, and I'm fighting with David at home. On top of all of that, my niece is calling, begging me to come to L.A. She says her mother, Nia, is acting weird. I've put off my niece long enough. I will have to make that sixty mile drive.

Nia has not been there for Mama or me. Although she's had a place, she would not let either of us live with her when we needed it. She became a Jehovah's Witness when she turned eighteen, which drove a huge wedge between us. We weren't very close to begin with, but now that Nia is a Jehovah's Witness, forget it. Mama and I are not Witnesses, so I suppose we're the devil's daughters.

Nia is on her second marriage and her third baby. She gave birth to a little boy and then had a girl two years later. Sadly, her son passed away from a fatal brain disorder when he was only five years old. Nia divorced and remarried, giving birth to a second baby girl when her eldest, Britt, was sixteen years old. Britt is sixteen-and-a-half now—old enough to stay in touch with Mama and me without her mother interfering.

~ ~ ~

While I am on my way to their place, Britt calls. She is asking me to hurry and get over there because her mother's "acting strange." Driving at top speed, I arrive quickly. Before pulling up to their house, I see that their front door is wide open.

"Hello, Britt?" I call out. No answer. Broken glass litters the floor. Curtains and shades are torn down. *What the hell is going on?* I'm tiptoeing through the house, nervous, afraid of what I may find. But it's empty. They're not here. *Where are they?*

As I reach the front yard, I see my niece standing on the corner and my sister halfway down the block. Nia and

Britt are facing each other, at a distance. It's a standoff. I sense that Britt has run there, scared of her.

"Oh, my God, Nia! What happened? What's going on?" I ask. But she's just staring at me, eyes wide, acting nervous.

"Nia? Who's Nia?" she asks.

"You!" *Oh no.* I can't get her to tell me what's wrong, so I head towards

Britt, who tries to hurry me up, yelling for me to get there faster.

"Mama's lost her mind, or something," she says. "A minute ago, her behavior seemed normal. The next minute, she was tearing down the curtains."

I make Britt follow me back to Nia.

"Nia, are you okay?" I ask her. No answer. She just keeps asking who I am and says she's never seen Britt or me in her life.

"Who is this girl?" she asks.

"This girl is Britt, your sixteen-year-old daughter," I tell her repeatedly. Nia keeps denying it, saying she didn't give birth to Britt but found her in a bloody bowl in the bathroom. *Oh, my God! Is this postpartum depression? Or schizophrenia?* I do a quick mental inventory of all the daytime TV shows I've ever watched, but I have no idea what to do. I've got to get her inside the house so I can figure out how to help her. I've got to call Mama.

By the time Mama pulls up with David, Nia has run across the street. Now she's standing in the middle of the park, praying loudly and walking in circles. She is acting very aggressive. I can't even get close to her.

Nia has gained a lot of weight over the years, and she is a big girl. She has always been on the weak side, but at this moment, she appears to possess the strength of ten. I'm not going to risk moving closer to her. Mama arrives and walks straight toward her, trying to convince her to go into the house.

"Who are you? Who are you?" Nia says as she pulls away from Mama. Mama looks at me as if to ask what's wrong. I can only shrug my shoulders.

None of us can get her into the house. Fortunately, firemen often park their trucks in front of her house to relax in the park. There are firemen there now. I go over to the fire trucks and ask the medics to help us take her into the house, but they have no authority to intervene. Instead, they call the police, asking them to help us.

When the policemen arrive, my sister looks at them the same way she looked at me. Her expression says, "Who are you? What are you doing here? Stay away from me!" She runs into the house.

The policemen take her to a psychiatric hospital. Even though Nia has committed no crime, they have to put her in handcuffs. We had a feeling they would, which is why we had wanted the medics to take her instead. This is heart wrenching. I'm so glad her baby is with her father and not here to see this. This is not my sister.

When we pick her up after a night in the hospital, Nia seems fine. She remembers everything that happened but doesn't know why she said the things she did. She just couldn't stop herself.

A few months pass and we get another phone call from Britt saying, "Come quick! The police are here again." This time, Nia's husband calls the police to take her away. He says he's afraid of her. He does not want her returning to the house. And she is forbidden to take the baby.

Nia and Britt are now staying with us. When my sister is home, she locks herself in the back bedroom. She leaves the house every day, only to come home late, reeking of urine. I decide to follow her one day in my car. I watch as Nia walks straight down Clark Boulevard—no turns, no pauses, just straight.

I drive away but return to see her still walking. *Where the hell is she going?* After doing this several times, I turn back.

Nia calls me at midnight from a phone booth. She says she is lost somewhere at the beach, and asks if I can find her and take her home. Within minutes, I'm in my car, driving up and down Pacific Coast Highway until I find her. Thank God I do.

Hours later, driving back home, Nia seems normal. She's always been a soft-spoken girl and that's the girl who's in the car with me now—thank God. Until she started having those yelling and screaming episodes, she was someone who would never raise her voice, or curse, or say a single bad thing about anyone. That's why seeing her flipped out like that was so shocking. She seemed possessed.

When we get home, she goes into the back room and shuts the door, shutting us out. Britt is worried. We all are.

As these episodes continue, Nia's husband tries to take her baby away from her. Mama says she won't let that happen, and goes to court to fight for visitation rights so my sister can have contact with her daughter.

It works. Mama wins visitation rights. The court order only allows my sister contact with her baby under my mother's supervision. Nia is not expressing anything verbally, but I know she's depressed about this restriction. On top of that, we learn that she may be going through psychotic episodes.

~ ~ ~

My marriage is becoming unbearable and with the added weight of having my family here, it is almost impossible for my husband and me to get on track.

He is a glory hog who craves praise every day and never wants me to get the recognition I deserve. I feel like he wants people to think I contribute only a bit of wifely inspiration to all the beautiful songs we create together.

He doesn't understand why that bugs the shit out of me. I am constantly having to remind people that I'm Peeps. "You remember? David's wife." *Am I that forgettable? Or does David just suck all the damn air out of a room?*

Our hateful words lead to knock-down, drag-out arguments and growing tension between us. David continues to fool himself, believing he's the mastermind behind our successful partnership. Reality, though, is screaming, "It's a joint effort!" Our relationship is beginning to sour.

~ ~ ~

We are in bad financial shape and no longer able to pay our bills. We purchased this house assuming our success was just beginning. David hasn't brought in any income in a few years. While I was dumping all my savings into my dream, he was being supportive, paying all the bills out of his savings.

We are forced to move off the hilltop where the affluent live, and return to a San Fernando Valley apartment. David's new black Cadillac Escalade is repossessed before our very eyes. I'm doing all I can to hold on to the Lexus.

Okay, now there's really no more money. *How is this happening? First, we lose the house. Now we're being evicted from the apartment. We've only been here a few months. We're published songwriters, for God's sake!* With no other alternatives, we eat our pride and decide to stay with friends.

~ ~ ~

"PK, can you please come pick me up at the Metro station?" Mama says with a slur at 2:00 a.m. I get small breaks from worrying about her, but the cloud is never far.

Mama, Nia and Britt are all living with a cousin. For the first time in a long while, Mama and I are separated. She is off drugs, but the alcohol is consistent. Mama always said that drugs were not a problem for her and that she could stop. I guess she was right. She hasn't used for a few years now; she says she doesn't miss it or crave it.

David suggests that he and his brother go live at a friend's place while I stay with someone else. This is very disturbing. His brother should return to Ohio and rejoin their mother and father. This would allow David and me—the married couple—some time and space to smooth out our relationship and find a way out of this mess.

But no, that's not David's vision. He absolutely does not want to separate from his brother. He and his younger brother are ten years apart in age, but extremely close. The age difference is a factor in David's immature behavior. He's living vicariously through his younger brother.

The two of them are together, staying with a friend, while I'm staying with a friend without my husband. This is the first time I've been separated from David since our marriage. My friend has kids and lives with her kids' father. I'm in the way while staying in their two-bedroom apartment. David and his brother are staying with a friend who is a bachelor with kids that stay with their mother. So they have space.

I've worn out my welcome. My cousin is housing my entire family, so I can't go there. I won't even tell them about this.

11

Just Shy of Skid Row

I'm homeless, sleeping in my car. It isn't easy living out of a car, especially for a woman. Something as routine as going to the bathroom becomes a daily challenge. I don't even want to think about that time of the month. I'm really getting creative here. I have dirty maxi pads in a plastic bag that I haven't even had a chance to throw out. That time of the month always seems to do something to my bowels too. Needing to wake up out of my sleep and dash to a gas-station bathroom is no easy task when my stomach is boiling over.

I shower at my friend's house when I'm sure I am not inconveniencing her. Most of the time I use sinks in public bathrooms. I try to find small restaurants that have bathrooms with only one stall and a lock on the door. I drive around all day in my house/writing suite. Before I was homeless, I would do my best writing in this car. I would turn the beat up loud and lose myself in the bass. I haven't written anything in a few weeks but I'm doing a lot of crying.

If I want to see David, I have to visit him at the apartment he's sharing. He asks about my night, and I want to strangle him. If looks could kill, he'd be dead.

My night? Full of terrifying people who are also alone and desperate to find refuge, a friend, or even a victim. They have been out here longer than I have and they would take what little I have because at least it would be more than what they have. Of course, I don't say this to him.

When he asks me if I'm scared, I say "No." I never really tell him how I feel about being out here. I shouldn't have to. Yes, I play tough and maybe that's why he doesn't show that much concern. He figures I can handle it. I've always been this way since I was a kid. I've developed a thick skin. Most of the guys I've been with seem to start off sweet, loving, and gentle with me. As time passes, their love morphs into toughness as they conclude I can handle anything and everything that comes my way. My sister used to think that about me when I was as young as six. She, too, believed I could handle more than she could.

"This music thing is not happening like we planned," I tell him. "I think we need to get little jobs at least. That way we can find an apartment, I can get off the street, and we can work on our marriage."

"Not me. I can't work a nine-to-five," he says.

"Even though your wife is sleeping in her car, starving? You're too good to work and earn money to support us?"

"Can't," he repeats.

Upset, I start the engine, telling him goodbye. He asks me to park in front of where he's staying so he can sleep out here in the car with me. He doesn't ask me to stay with him in his nice, warm, comfortable bed—not even for one damn night. I'm furious.

I tell him no, I will be fine, I'll try and sleep over at my friend's—the one who lets me shower at her house. I don't mean a word of it. I just want him out of the car. I am too disgusted and disappointed to be around him tonight.

He grabs four dollars out of his pocket and hands it to me. I go to the grocery store and buy water and two cups of noodles. They're the easiest and most convenient thing to prepare without a kitchen. I can always go into 7–11 and use their hot water to cook my noodles. I can't tell you how many of these I've eaten in the fifty-two days I've been out here.

Only two other people know about my situation. Well, they think they do. I gave them only half the story. They don't know that I sleep in the street at night.

~ ~ ~

Tonight is crazy. There seems to be drama happening on every corner. I really need to sleep in a safer area, but

I don't have money for gas. I need to stay within easy distance of David. A loud crash wakes me up. It's barely morning, and the sun is just rising. *What the hell was that noise?*

Damn! Somebody busted my front passenger window. I don't even look around to see who might be responsible. I hop over my front seat, struggle to get the car keys out of my jeans pocket, start the car, and take off as fast as I can.

Okay, that's it. I drive straight to the Del Amo Mall. I'm running on fumes the whole way, praying I'll make it. When I get there, I fill out an application for employment. Once hired, I'm at work every day. I don't let anyone know about my situation—not my coworkers and definitely not my friends and colleagues in the music business. If my colleagues know I am homeless, working retail in a mall, it will not look good. I have to keep up appearances and fake it 'til I make it.

Even in my current situation, I am determined to get Maze a spot on Billboard's Top 100. I hit the music scene every night, sleep in the car, and report to work every morning. Our store is the number-one store in sales. We are very popular with the wealthy housewives in this upscale part of town. It's my job to convince them that the clothes are beautiful—and they are too. It's exhausting to run around for eight hours a day, dressing fussy ladies who all hate different parts of their bodies. And it's nerve-wracking having no access to an iron and limited access to a shower when all the clients and my coworkers are so well put together. I'm fully aware that with the amount of money these women have, either I'm great at the job or I'm out.

~ ~ ~

Today is a busy day. Our number-one sales girl is up to twenty thousand dollars in sales. I'm number two at eleven thousand dollars. I could have sold more but I didn't get a chance to shower last night. All I got was a once-over in the McDonald's bathroom sink this morning. So, I'm not feeling my best. *Can the customers see the bottom of my feet when I walk in my sling-backs? They're not too clean right now.*

At the end of the shift, we close in pairs and walk each other out. I know who will be closing with me, and where they park, and I park as far away as I can. I don't want her seeing the mountain of clothes in my car. Then I drive to a nice street in this neighborhood—a place where I feel safe. The truth is, I'm never safe when I'm sleeping on the streets.

My first paycheck isn't much. The only thing it covers is my car note. David is extremely pissed that I choose to use my paycheck to make my car payment. He tells me I should let the car be repossessed. He refuses to work, and wants me to give up the car that I sleep in, the car that provides transportation to work every day, so I can spend the money I'm earning on things he considers necessities.

I work so we can eat and hopefully one day get out of this mess. We're constantly arguing about this, but I will not bend on this one. It's an insane argument. He and his brother have a warm place to stay and I do not.

I continue pleading with him to find work, but he refuses. His brother won't work either. David is acting like he is too good to take a job after being somewhat successful in the music business. I try to get him to see that this success is new for him, and so is this town, this industry. I'm the one who's lived in the entertainment capital of the world my whole life, been in the faces of some well-to-do people, and had my own level of success. But I'm not embarrassed to work out here. So he sure as hell could, being that no one really even knows him yet. It's useless. Not even my best argument will convince him to get a damn job and help out.

My best friend has two kids, and they both move to Arkansas to go to school. So, she allows me to stay with her. She has a place in the heart of L.A. in a not-so-bad but not-so-good neighborhood. I pay half the rent. Sometimes she lets David and his brother sleep over, but she can't let them live here. The landlord won't allow them to stay indefinitely. I now have a place to lay my head and a chance to get my life and marriage back on track.

Speaking of my marriage, I'm trying to really pay attention. The way David is behaving during the worst time of our lives together says a lot about him. I feel like I am one second shy of a complete breakdown.

~ ~ ~

Mama needs to borrow the car to take Grandma to an important doctor's appointment, so she drops me off at work today. As I watch her pull away, I have a very uncomfortable feeling in the pit of my stomach. Within minutes of leaving work, I'm almost bursting with the anxiety that dogged me all day. I can't seem to shake it. When I have premonitions about Mama's welfare, something bad is usually on the way. Sometimes it has already arrived.

Mama is late. She's supposed to be here by now. And she isn't answering her cell phone.

"She left around seven o'clock," Grandma says when I call her.

It's 9:00 p.m. now. The mall where I work is only a twenty-five-minute drive from Grandma's house. I call Mama's cell phone about a thousand times over the next hour. Now that feeling in my stomach is so strong that I actually puke. *This mall is very hard to navigate. Mama could be lost, circling the mall's enormous parking lot.* This thought is the only thing keeping me together.

It's 11:00 pm. Two hours have passed since I spoke to Grandma, and I have covered every inch of the parking structure. Security guards stop and ask if I'm okay. I know in my soul that something is wrong.

I call Grandma again. I don't want to worry her, but I need more information.

"Has she been drinking, Grandma?" I ask.

"I think so," she says hesitantly, not wanting me to worry. "Was she drunk?"

Grandma explains that she can't always be sure if Mama's been drinking. She didn't see her drinking, but yes, she believes so.

I'm angry with her. "Why did you let her drive in that condition?" I ask harshly, and hang up. I've never expressed such anger towards Grandma in my life.

I wonder who else I can call. I can't call David for help because he doesn't even have a car. *Where are Mama's two older brothers—my uncles?* They have been absent my whole life and have never given much thought to my sister and me. They may be disgusted by Mama's behavior, but we need them.

I don't want to do this, but I have to call Reign. He agrees to come, but he's an hour from here. I work in Redondo Beach and he's in Canoga Park, on the opposite side of the world. That's fine. That will give me time to comb the mall one more time. *Mama must be lost somewhere close by.*

I'm walking around, almost falling to my knees from worry. Fear sends terrible signals throughout my body. I know she's hurt. *Oh, Lord! Please protect my mother.* I pray out loud, repeatedly. It's around midnight when Reign pulls up. I'm exhausted from walking and worrying. I can barely speak. Sinking deep into his passenger's seat, I express my fears, and tell him I know Mama must be hurt. He calms me down enough to call Nia.

"She's probably okay. Just call me when you find her," she tells me.

This gives me no comfort. I know Mama would never leave me if something weren't drastically wrong. I call one my cousins in Long Beach. She is my mother's favorite niece, and we have been close my entire life. She loves my mother very much, and is almost as close to her as I am. She immediately wakes up and starts crying. She promises to call the California Highway Patrol to ask if there's been an accident reported southbound on the 405.

Reign and I reach Grandma's apartment and go inside. The place is extremely small. She has a collage on her wall that Mama made for her out of pictures of all of Grandma's children and grandchildren over the years. She has a small couch, a TV that sits on a small stand, and her favorite blue-checkered recliner that sits next to her living room window. It's always so hot in here.

I find a high school picture of Mama, and stare into her big brown eyes. All I see is a good girl who had dreams and great ideals until she met my father and those eyes went dark.

I can tell that Grandma is worried, and ashamed of herself for allowing Mama to drive drunk. She keeps trying to convince me not to worry, and speculates that Mama must have stopped at a friend's house. She says, "Or, maybe she drank too much and passed out."

I know that Mama would never stop at a friend's

house, leaving me to worry and wait for her until midnight. We're too close for that. She isn't that kind of a mother. Even when she is drunk, she always shows up.

"Something bad happened, Grandma. I feel it."

I remember an evening some years earlier, when Reign and I were on our way out to a movie. I had a strong feeling that Mama was in distress, and asked him to take me to my mother right away. He thought I was crazy to insist out of the blue, but I was adamant. When I got home, she was lying on the floor, choking on some chewing gum. I had to help her spit it up. If I'd ignored that feeling, she might have choked to death. That was Reign's lesson. It was the last time he doubted my premonitions about my mother.

It is now 2:00 a.m. My cousin calls back and tells me that no accidents have been reported southbound on the 405. Grandma is asleep with her head back on the chair. Reign's eyes are closed too, as he dozes on the couch. But the fear running through my head won't allow me to close mine. My cell phone rings.

"Hello," I answer, already in tears.

"Are you Billie King?" a woman asks.

"Yes."

"This is Cathy from Cedars-Sinai. We have your mother here."

I don't hear anything else she says. I'm out the door, heading to Cedars-Sinai Hospital. I get to the emergency room. A cop stands by the door of the examining room where they have Mama. "Your mother was in a terrible car accident on Coldwater Canyon," he tells me.

Why was she way over there? That's north. She has no friends in the Valley.

"She was in an accident. Her car flipped over three times, landed on its hood, and slid into an embankment. Lucky for her and others, there were no other cars involved. She hit the side of the mountain at top speed, and it flipped the car. They had to cut her out. She's lucky to be alive."

Very slowly, I walk behind the curtain of the examining room. The room reeks of alcohol. She's lying there with her head strapped down. The blood from her wounds is caked onto her hands and saturating her clothes. I can't hold it together. I break down, sobbing. The cop comes in.

"She was lucky. Another car tumbled over the same embankment a few months earlier and exploded," he says.

The nurse tells me that Mama has four broken ribs and many scrapes and bruises, but that's it. Mama wakes up and starts crying. Unable to move her head or arms, she reaches for me, saying how sorry she is about the car, which she knows I loved. But all I can think about is how happy I am that she's still alive.

I see her heart rate starting to climb on the monitor, so I calm her down the way I always have. I climb into the emergency room bed and wrap my arms around her so she'll go to sleep. The next day, the hospital transfers Mama to a new room.

I go to claim the car. It's crushed like a soda can. I can't believe that Mama not only survived the crash, but also escaped it with so few injuries.

I call David to tell him what happened to Mama. He says he'll try to come to the hospital to see her the next day. But three days pass, and he never shows up. I can never lean on him in a crisis.

~ ~ ~

Mama spends months recuperating at my cousin's house. She's been on permanent disability for several years since falling off a thirty-foot ladder while drunk and trying to climb through a window. She crushed her heel and shattered the bone in her left elbow that day. To avoid embarrassing conversations, I tell friends that she fell off a ladder while working at Howard Hughes, an aircraft company. She actually worked there for a while, on the assembly line, many years ago and not for very long.

Mama has lived with me in every house I've rented since I became an adult. She stayed with me for a short time when I lived with Reign, and later when I lived with David. Yep, both men knew they couldn't have me without accepting my bond with my mother. I don't have a place of my own right now, and I thank God for my cousin.

While Mama is recuperating, my relationship with David is quickly coming to an end. He is still staying with his friend, and seems to be perfectly comfortable without a wife. I beg him to let me see him, but each plea is met with flimsy excuses.

He finally comes to the house where I'm staying to tell me that he'll be returning to Ohio for Thanksgiving. "I'll be back before Christmas." Christmas comes and goes. David tells me he'll return to L.A. before the year is out, but I bring in the New Year without him.

As the weeks pass, David's transparent lies continue. He claims that he landed several gigs in Ohio and says he'll come back when they're finished. Finally, after running out of every other excuse, he tells me, "I want to stay out here a little longer, for my son."

There's no way to oppose his decision without him accusing me of being a selfish, mean woman who's trying to keep him from his son. I wanted kids and we tried for many years. It happened once, but I lost it at nine weeks. I had too much stress in my life to hold a baby. *Is that why he doesn't consider us a real family? Is that why he can walk off and leave me for so long?*

Six months pass, and then a year. I now know that he'll never come home to me. He's gone. That's the hard, cold reality.

12

Larceny

It's been over two years since David left. Mama's managed to get her own place with Nia and Britt. And I am finally getting my life together, and moving on without my husband. I have a new apartment and a new miniature Yorkshire Terrier named Brownee. I even have a new BMW, thanks to Ames, the clothing store where I worked, and a pretty healthy licensing deal on the overseas music rights for the songs I wrote with David.

Things are looking brighter, but my heart is still shattered. The abandonment by my husband is too much for me to handle. I'm coming up with crazy ideas—like tattooing a big mural on my back and coloring my hair bright red. I want to go all the way out and make a *fuck-you* statement to the world. But what would my grandmother think? I would never be able to see her again without her being disgusted. And what about Mama? She is against tattoos, and doesn't even like me wearing a lot of makeup. She'd give me hell for a tattoo, I know. But to hell with everybody; they're not the ones in pain.

I'm pumped up. A couple of shots of tequila will numb the sting of the needle. *Shit, whom am I kidding?* My mural is going to take a whole bottle of Cuervo Gold.

"What does that symbol stand for?"

"Pain," he says.

"Perfect. I'll take that one." My mural goes from a skyline with broken hearts and destruction to a little symbol on the small of my back representing exactly what I feel: *pain*.

Speaking of pain, David swears he hasn't abandoned me. I guess he feels that if he keeps in touch almost every day, it's not abandonment. I believe it's his way of keeping me under his spell even though he's not here. It's working. I can't move on.

I intend to go hard on my career this year. I need the distraction. Now I know why some artists write their biggest songs after heartbreak. The lyrics and melodies flow out of you like tears. Mine are hard, underground raps with dark bass lines, loud claps, and high hats. I'm angry and I can't shed another tear. There are none left.

I believed that David was the final resting place for me. I never wanted to be with another man. Now that damn cloud is trying to cover me. It's no longer beside me. It's on top of me and it's dark. I can barely figure out the path or understand how to get there.

~ ~ ~

I feel closed in and I need a release. Music is the only place I feel freedom. A friend, Fam, invites me down to the studio where he's recording his next album. He wants to get me on a song with him, and introduce me to someone he calls Oakland, who he thinks can help me. Fam was mainstream back in the day, but now he speaks for the heartbeat of the streets, which is what moves me most.

Fam is a street rapper. To my way of thinking, gangster rap is different than street rap. Gangsters talk about killing, drugs, and dirty money, but street rappers speak for the people of the ghetto, of their pain and struggle. It's dark but it has depth and truth. That's my style. That's what makes my blood warm.

I hear that Fam's friend, Oakland (real name Damon) is a UCLA graduate who's been in the music business almost since he graduated over fifteen years ago. He's in radio as the assistant program director for a radio station—the number-one station for the past six years. Fam describes Damon as an honest guy, and says that with all his connections and experience, he can help me make it to the next level.

Fam knows I've been talking about moving to the

East Coast, just to get away and start fresh with my debut artist, Maze. But he's from there, and doesn't think I have the balls (figuratively speaking) to hack it out there. He is hoping that Damon can give me what I need to help me stay on the West Coast.

After guest appearing on a song with Fam, Damon walks in. Fam was right—we hit it off, and from that night on, he helps me with the launch of my label.

I'm still working on getting my own album out through my company. I have everything I want, minus the rock-star status. That's cool. I'm coming in through the back door as an Executive Producer.

My record label is now official. I hire the most skilled production professionals to assist with ensuring that Maze's record does well. Leaving no stone unturned, I even hire Damon as GM and head of radio promotions. This addition makes my team as strong as steel.

Even with all the good that is happening, I am still unable to forget about David. In trying to get over David, I've become sexually involved with Damon. I know that this is not a good idea, and could even be disastrous, but my mind and body need the escape.

Damon is a Raiders season-ticket holder. Despite my reservations, I agree to go. Damon also mentions a club he wants to take me to. It's some kind of sex club in San Francisco called the Power Exchange. The way I've been feeling lately, I am willing to do just about anything.

A couple of men wearing leather and chains and a woman in a rubber nurse's uniform and twelve-inch platform boots duck through the door ahead of us. I grab a handful of assorted condoms from the bowl next to the cash register while Damon pays a middle-aged woman, who avoids eye contact. We have been talking about this for days, and the excitement is like a high-voltage current burning between us. One of the men ahead of us slips on a leather mask while his partner snaps a leash to it. This crowd is not what I expected.

"You came on the wrong night," someone in line says after hearing me complaining. We thought it was couples' night and planned to spice things up a bit. This is way out of our comfort zone. We have never been to any club like this. Honestly, we didn't think black people would frequent a sex club, period. Usually our culture is just not that freaky. But I find some silent comfort in seeing the other black couple in line.

It turns out that it's not couples' night. It is fetish night. On one floor, couples sex each other while we watch—and that's not bad. But down a level, it's different. A man is being whipped with a cat-o'-nine-tails. His back and ass are as red as my nail polish. A woman in a schoolgirl skirt is being beaten with a paddle, and a naked guy is stretched out on some kind of medieval torture device, with a big weight hanging from his balls. Past that is a row of TVs playing porn. A fleshy white man—and I do mean white—stands in front, jacking off.

I feel like I'm in hell. I'm holding onto Damon very tight. He's not that tall—five feet eleven inches—but strong and muscular, secure and safe.

"Get me out of here!" I plead. The devil is all over this place.

Damon got an older friend who's a regular in this club to go with us. We finally leave, but the friend and his date—who is not his wife—decide to stay.

Back at the hotel room, I'm not feeling very turned on—more like disturbed. Damon tries to convince me that it was just the wrong night and we need to go back on couples-only night. It doesn't take long after showering until I'm turned on again. We screw like rabbits for what feels like all night. We finally fall asleep, wake up, and do it again.

"You okay?" he asks after I return a phone call from David that I took in the bathroom. He has been pretty understanding about things. David continues to haunt me with his phone calls. It's still, without question, abandonment, but he knows the calls will keep me weak for him. Why do I give him the satisfaction?

I crawl back into bed and show Damon just how okay I am. I climb on top of him to straddle his strong, lean body. Slow and easy, I pump up and down, around and around. He goes deeper as I grind down on him, slowly bringing him to ecstasy.

We're climaxing at the same time. I release all my stress and anguish onto his pelvis while he explodes deep inside me. He falls asleep with that innocent grin, and I stare into the darkness.

~ ~ ~

The night before, the owner of the club told us to give it another try and go back the next evening for couples' night. We decide to do it. This time, though, we're going alone. I pick out clothes for Damon. *No, not the fresh white T-shirt he always wears.* For me, I choose a miniskirt and black thigh-high tights—for easy access.

This is the right night to be here. I'm turned on as I walk around, watching couples having sex directly in front of me. As we leave the club, I immediately feel shy again.

"Oh, my goodness! Did that just happen, babe?" I say. We laugh out loud and quickly leave the club. Exhausted, we head to his friends' house to spend our last night.

I'm sleeping in one room. Damon is sleeping alone on the couch to show respect for their kids. I'm so horny. Something about being alone in this room while he's in the other room away from me makes me want him. He must be feeling the same way because he's crawling into bed with me.

"I'm thinking of how wet you were in that club," he says. I put his hand into my panties so he can feel how wet I am now. Having sex while trying to be quiet with the family in the other room has me climaxing harder than I ever have before—hard enough to lose myself in this amazing sexual chemistry we have.

Is it that? Or is he just a way to escape and release from all the pain?

I'm not that proud of the Power Exchange. I realize I have hit an all-time low. I've done some pretty unbelievable things with Damon while also trying to be as honest as I can about this ever turning into a relationship. He says he is completely fine with that.

~ ~ ~

By now we've completed Maze's album, and it reaches an audience of forty-four million. We've shot the video, which is playing on BET, VH1, Video Soul, and several local video stations. The single is playing on several Radio 1 and Clear Channel stations, and more than one of our songs is on the Billboard Top 100. The public is really responding to Maze. I hope this will give David some inspiration. If he sees that I can do it, maybe he'll learn that he can too.

My company is a small boutique label. I have to wear a million hats. I'm not just the owner. I'm the head of the front office, I answer the phones, I do mail-outs, and I lick stamps. I am the director, the producer—you name it. My motto is, *No job too large or small.*

Damon feels that because he's older, he knows more. It could be true about some things, but I've been in this business since I was eighteen and I know a little something about it. Damon is challenging me every day. If I say that Maze should go right, he says he should go left. If I say I want the staff to meet every week on Wednesdays, he says we should meet on Tuesdays. If I ask him to make a run to the post office, he says, "That's not my job."

It is not my job either but I make it happen.

Damon really is a nice guy who I've always been able to talk to. But he has failed to persuade me to be a real couple, and I still see who I want to see. He initially said he was fine with that, but now he is being a little vindictive.

"Can I talk to you for a minute?" I ask him.

He agrees to meet for a drink after we leave the office.

"Thank you for coming," I say. Then I ask him what I can do to make life easier for both of us in the workplace. I reiterate how I want to find a middle ground where we can have peace. He's agitated and aggravated—no longer the soft-spoken guy I remember. He leaves me hanging on for a solution that never comes. I throw back my shot of Cuervo Gold and watch him walk out the door.

It seems that men try to control everything I am and everything I do. They want to control my happiness, my freedom, and my financial independence. Just the thought of a man can sometimes feel constricting.

~ ~ ~

This is an exciting time for my label and Maze. Maze is invited to perform at an annual event in New York City, and the team and I set up radio and magazine interviews. But Damon is being standoffish on the trip. He has his nose in his Blackberry for two hours, trying to avoid eye contact. *This dude can't do it. He can't be professional. Okay, cool. Whatever keeps the drama down.*

We have a rooftop meeting with the editor of a top magazine. On the way up in the elevator, Maze grabs the camera out of my hand and starts to film the awkward silence between Damon and me. Damon says something disrespectful on camera, but before I can reply, the elevator doors open and we are greeted on the rooftop by the editor.

Damon set up this interview. Instead of introducing me to the editor as the owner of the company, he says, "This is Billie." No title—not even my last name.

On the flight back to L.A., I am in deep thought. I will have to put an end to this. Damon and I are getting into crazy arguments, and it's starting to wear me down. This should be one of the happiest and most rewarding times of my life, but I'm spending it defending myself against accusations of selfishness. I can't deal with Damon.

Maze is not just my artist—he's also a close friend. His mother, who is his biggest supporter and my spiritual advisor, has mentioned on more than one occasion that I am the only other woman on this planet that she trusts with her son. I hold that dear. I will not let either one of them down. I tell Maze that I have to let Damon go as general manager of the label because he's a cancer I can no longer handle. I describe our conflict and explain what has been causing our disputes. Maze says he has confidence in Damon's abilities to handle radio promotions. He believes Damon will be able to get the record moving up in rotation.

I agree and feel that it is my best chance at success in radio. I ask Damon to resign as general manager, but to stay on as an independent contractor in radio promotions. He is unhappy with the decision but says he'll consider my offer. The next day, he tells me he's going to sue me.

"Well, bring it on!" I've been fighting my whole life. What's one more fight?

Damon has no grounds for a suit. I paid him every month for radio promotions. He and I agreed that if the relationship started to go south early in the process, he would simply leave. If he'd been able to keep his personal feelings out of it, we could have made things work. *I swear, I have the worst luck with men.*

The number-one personality in radio invites Maze and the label heads to an awards show he puts on every year in Vegas. He sets up all the accommodations, and we head out. He is one of our biggest supporters, but it didn't start out that way. Although he and Maze go way back—to Maze's childhood, in fact—we had to convince him that Maze's music should speak for itself. He and his manager were skeptical about Maze, believing that he would mess up the opportunity. Or as he said, "Maze gets in his own way." But when we played the music, they couldn't deny his talent.

Maze is scheduled to present the awards and to perform at the after-party. We're on our way out to the sound check, waiting for Maze to come downstairs. *Wait, who is that? What the hell is Damon doing here?* He walks up and stands by the car, talking to my assistant and radio-promotions person. *Is he trying to get in the car?*

I ask to speak to him for a moment. "What are you doing here?" I ask him. Looking straight into my eyes, he says, "Don't you know?"

"Know what?"

"I'm managing Maze now," he says.

Maze was my friend before I ever introduced him to Damon. I ask Damon what the hell he's talking about, and say, "Maze is broke! I've been giving him money every week. I know you're low on money, and your contacts don't always pan out. How are you going to be able to help him?" I ask.

"Maze and I got this," he says and climbs into the car I'm paying for. Suddenly Maze shows up and jumps into the car without saying a word.

I'm furious. This is an ambush. Maze and Damon sit in the back while I'm fuming in the passenger seat. I need to hold in my anger for now. I can't show my ass in public, so to speak. If I lash out, that will give them all they need to brand me "an emotional, unprofessional bitch." This is such a great moment for Maze and my label. I will not give Damon that satisfaction.

Damon is actually overseeing Maze's sound check. *Am I being punked? Where are the fucking cameras?* I know Maze wouldn't hire Damon to manage his career after I fired him, especially since this man is now threatening to sue me. *Who does that?* I told him Damon was like a cancer. *What in the hell is Maze thinking?*

The sound check is over.

"Maze, how could you ambush me like this when you know the deal?" "It's my life," he says. Maze bonded with Damon on a trip I did not take with them. It was the one and only time I stayed behind. Damon took that opportunity to poison Maze against me and now he wants him to be his manager. I tell Maze that Damon won't be able to advance his career, that he's not a closer. "Damon knows influential people because he worked for the radio station for six years, but he's never been able to close a deal since I've known him. It was not until I gave him some money to throw around that they took a meeting. Furthermore, he's feuding with your label's CEO—your friend and biggest supporter."

So far, I've bet three hundred thousand dollars on making Maze relevant. And before leaving for Las Vegas, Maze and I spoke about several potential managers who could take him to the next level. I'm a new company. It only makes sense to get a manager with a reputation to help position his project. As a reward for my kindness, Maze has spit in my face with this whole management situation.

It's hard to accept. Nothing I or anyone else can say has any effect. Maze refuses to part with Damon, who is now his manager. I remind Maze that I will not be communicating with Damon in any way. I hadn't done so for months before Maze's decision, and I won't be doing so now.

~ ~ ~

After failing to find work through Damon, Maze is eventually cast in a play on Broadway. Finally, he has the opportunity to give back to the one who gave so much to him. I need it right now in the worst way. In fact, he's contractually obligated to me for a small portion of his earnings from music and acting. However, he refuses to comply with the terms of our agreement. Instead he's upset with me!

Contractually, I'd fulfilled my obligations—I gave him twenty thousand dollars, shot a video, and got him radio play and tour support. He was broke and needed more help, so I moved him from Harlem to Los Angeles. I figured if he was close by, I could help him more easily. I put him in an apartment rent-free, and gave him one hundred dollars a week for food.

Once Maze brought in Damon to manage him, I told them both that I'd done my part and would not continue with Maze's day-to-day living expenses—that would now be his manager's responsibility. They said, "Cool."

But, when Damon failed to get Maze any paying gigs, he ended up having to sleep on a friend's couch, and blamed me for no longer being able to freeload.

He spit in my face—the one person who believed in him for all those years—then became upset that everything wasn't working out for him. I can see what the radio personality manager meant by "Maze always manages to get in his own way."

Before Maze got the Broadway role and refused to comply with our agreement, I'd been negotiating a distribution deal with a reputable record label that has several hits under their belts. The label's CEO loved Maze's message as well as his album. He loved the material we came up with for the record. It was a long few months of negotiations, during which the label agreed to give me the money I put in plus marketing money. Maze wanted a lot but refused to give up much for it. I spent three months negotiating this deal and at the last minute, Maze blew the deal by being unreasonable.

I can't let it go that easily, and I'm back in the fight to save it. I salvage the deal and get everything straightened out, only to find out that Maze sent a long email behind my back, essentially saying, "Thanks, but no thanks."

Maze has no right to send emails to the company without my knowledge, while I'm in negotiations with them. This was a chance to really make some money from my investment of time, money and effort—and for him to cement some stardom with his music. He blew it, and it feels like he did it on purpose.

With no joint venture deal, and no income coming in for me from the play, I'm running out of time and options. I've already spent three hundred thousand dollars. I have to let all my employees go until I'm able to restart operations, if such a thing is even possible. What is even more painful is that Maze wants to ditch the company. He is ready to leave me high and dry after my complete dedication to him and his career.

~ ~ ~

I haven't seen or heard from Damon or Maze for an entire year. Maze dissed me for Damon, based on Damon's claims that he could take Maze to the next level, but it's been awfully uneventful for Maze. *Karma is a bitch.*

Damon is still working in radio, and Maze had to return to the East Coast for a while because nothing was happening. Enough said.

One evening I run into Damon at a recording studio. *What a joke, running into him here!* There were several ways I pictured running into Damon. All of them played out with a 9-1-1 call made over me trying to kill him. But all I feel is calmness.

Damon calls and emails after the encounter at the studio. He apologizes repeatedly. He sends me long emails explaining his take on what happened back then and why. He pleads with me to forgive him. What I haven't told him is that my issue was more with Maze than with him. Maze was someone I considered a friend. My heart is hardened at this point. I know people make mistakes and I've made a million of them, but I am not ready to forgive him. I'm not sure I'll ever be.

"Inhale
1,2,3,4,5
Exhale
6,7,8,9,10
Breathe Girl"

13

Before I Let Go

The pain of David leaving me is subsiding. If I had cut myself with a large knife, it wouldn't compare to what I had been feeling.

I never stopped working on Nsomnia Kafe and writing songs for placement. Kafe is going strong. The lyrical content of the songs is incredible. I get Kafe's music to an A&R guy for Aftermath. The A&R guy loves us and wants Dr. Dre to sign us. He needs an undeniable smash hit before he'll make the connection. So he hooks us up with a producer who also works with Busta Rhymes, and he produces two track mixes for us. We give him a hot bonus track—making it three tracks instead of two—and he immediately takes the tracks to Dre.

"They don't like us strong,

They like us dumb in a thong…

So I shakka my ass…droppa my pants and do him all night long…

You have to picture that chorus spoken with a sexy Asian accent. DOPE! But Dr. Dre turns it down. I wonder if he has something against rappers from the West Coast.

Some time passes. Now Dr. Dre is holding auditions, looking for a solo female rapper. A slew of female rappers show up, including me. It's insane how my professional life has unfolded. I've written for platinum artists, and become my own boss by launching my own label with some local success. But, now I am back where I started, trying to get an artist deal.

We are all in the studio, waiting to go into the booth and freestyle to this beat. It's my turn. I am in the recording booth with my heart beating fast. *Oh no! Am I about to have a panic attack right here, right now? Inhale 1,2,3,4,5, exhale 6,7,8,9,10. Breathe, girl.*

"Are you ready?"

I'm unsure of myself. Am I going to make it through this? I close my eyes and go hard. I rhyme to the first beat. Then they ask me to go again to a different, slower beat. They ask none of the girls who go before me to do this—I'm the only one. They call me back at the end of the audition.

"We choose you," his producers say, "but we have to let Dre hear it."

I've got a bad feeling about this. Remember, he didn't seem to be feeling us West Coast rappers. Dre chooses a chick from Philly. He disses the West Coast yet again.

There was one major victory here today. I was able to stop a panic attack in a matter of minutes. That means I've pretty much eradicated the attacks, and I'm proud of myself for that accomplishment. What I'm feeling at this moment is the need to regroup, to figure out my next move.

I know that stress is what triggers the attacks. This business, when it's proving hard to penetrate, is stress on top of more stress. Maybe I'm looking at the whole thing the wrong way, thinking that the music business is going to save my life. The truth is, music has already saved my life. The business part of it is trying to destroy my love for the music.

I think back…there's my father performing around the house, singing into his comb…Mama making percussion out of uncooked rice and a plastic bottle…a young me playing music with spoons, envisioning my girl band touring the world, exploring…rapping in front of a crowd of my peers for the first time, and them liking me…selling a song. It wasn't about the money—it was about them actually liking it enough to buy it.

I should've run away, far way, gone away from here… I should've run away, far away, gone away from here. Time keeps on ticking ticking…

Gotta get away before I grab it, click and spray... No more holidays, just keeping hope days,

All day toke and choke days, boy girl drama soap days, Full of broke days...

But I can't raise...I stick like PostIts... Gotta grind to keep the Coast up, Can't stop get my dose up...

My hustle excites me, but it ruins me like porn...

And if I drop from the grind, just don't forget to mourn.

~ ~ ~

I need to call Tiny. She's been calling for weeks, trying to take me out to get my mind off of things. No answer. I need to get out and do something. Who can I call? No, I am not calling Anthony. He was much too aggressive.

When we went out, I spent our first date fending off his advances. I swore to never see him again. He shoved his tongue down my throat, and wouldn't keep his hands off me. He must have been told that black girls put out because he was on me as though I was supposed to like it.

I'm bored, maybe even looking for a little trouble. I decide to give him another chance. This will be my first time dating outside my race. Anthony has the most beautiful dark brown eyes. He has wavy black hair and thick dark— but not too dark—eyebrows. He's tall, dark, handsome, and always manicured. The only thing missing is that shadowy beard that Italian models have. In his line of work, which is real estate, he has to be clean-shaven.

He has only been in the States for five years, so he still has a thick Italian accent. I like strong, powerful men, and that he definitely is. He wears custommade suits and ties, more tapered than I like, but I know it's the Euro look. At six-foot-two-inches tall, he towers over me. You can tell he has nicely built legs. He explains that he got them when he used to play hockey in his country.

I've always dated men with little or no money. I thought that girls who only went out with men for money were pathetic. My thought process is a little different now. This is my opportunity to experience a different race, and the money doesn't hurt. If only I could tame his aggressive behavior.

~ ~ ~

Anthony never lets me forget how I put him off his game. He says he's usually a strong, assertive man. But he followed me around the entire club when he first laid eyes on me, and could not muster up the courage to speak to me. He had to send someone over. Now he's doing everything in his power to sweep me off my feet. It's working. We take out the Jet Ski every weekend. We roll around in Bentleys, Porsches, and BMWs. His favorite car is his Presidential BMW 7 Series. We put many miles on it, never sitting still.

I'm not completely comfortable with how much—and how fast—he likes me. I do not feel that way for him. I feel like he smothers me.

I deserve this lifestyle, I tell myself. On the other hand, this could be seen as low-grade prostitution. Sometimes I'm mean right after he gives me a gift. He can't understand the behavior. I get mad at myself for being so damn weak. He knows he's trying to buy my love, and I'm letting it happen.

As he drives, he takes my arm and kisses it from fingertip to shoulder. He's constantly staring at me, which is extremely uncomfortable. He says he's always wanted to date a black girl, but he never imagined that she would be as beautiful and classy as I am.

I don't feel all that classy. People always thought I was from a different country, a whole different part of the world, because of the way I dress and carry myself. It may also be because of my mixed look from Mama's half-Irish side and my father's Creole side. But when all is said and done, I'm a black girl from Compton.

Anthony shows up at my apartment with a hundred-and-fifty-thousand-dollar check.

"This is for you," he says. "A little cushion so you don't have to work, and we can spend more time together."

I am not all about some love shit. Anthony is showing me something different, and I see no reason not to pay attention. He wants to move me into a better apartment.

I've always loved Hancock Park; it's where all the very expensive homes are between L.A. and Hollywood. It's a perfect location.

I find a beautiful duplex owned by the daughter of a famous, old-school guitar player. It's really something how I'm never too far from music. She's asking thirty-five hundred dollars a month.

"In order to move me there, you have to put a year of rent in my account," I say to Anthony. I do not trust men at this point of my life. David messed that up for me. *How will I be able to afford this if he leaves me?* Yes, I have the one hundred and fifty thousand, but if I get a year's cushion of rent on top of that, then I won't need him or any other man for that matter. He agrees. I'm in my beautiful duplex in Hancock Park and spending all my free time with him.

~ ~ ~

Anthony has a loft downtown but spends most of his nights in Hancock Park with me. He's getting too comfortable; my whole coat closet is full of his suits. He gets upset if I ask him to go home for a little while. Since David, I have no desire to share a home with a man. I express this to Anthony when he tells me he wants to give up his loft and stay here with me. I get him to let it go for now.

He is getting clingy. He's unable to be without me. Even when he goes into his office, he has me go with him.

I hate going there with him. He's turned his whole staff against me by making them wait on me hand on foot. That isn't his intention—he's just trying to show me how much he loves me and how much he wants me to be comfortable. But that's what happens. I'm not used to this kind of treatment, although I have to admit I'm starting to like it.

Anthony is more like me than any man I've been with before him. I even forget that we're from different parts of the world until we pass a mirror together and I'm reminded. I can't say that I love him, but I am very fond of his commitment to me.

I'm not open or honest enough with him to tell him my real age. I have three years on him. I don't feel comfortable letting him in on my issues with Mama. And I don't let him know that I'm from Compton, not some exotic foreign location. I'm sure in his country, he only heard negative things about Compton. He dug into my background and learned that my great-grandmother was from Calcutta, India. It seems he latched onto that, and now he tells everyone I'm Bollywood.

~ ~ ~

Anthony buys me a black, convertible Mercedes-Benz and takes me shopping at Ames for my birthday. The ladies I worked with while I was homeless and sleeping in my car are now fighting over who will have me as a client.

I roll around in this beautiful car for months until suddenly, I am being asked by the police to turn off the engine, get out, and step away from the vehicle? *Pulled over in Beverly Hills. How embarrassing is that?*

"What is going on?" I ask the officer. No answer.

Now the cops are all spread out, standing in pairs, and the black cops on my left side are staring oddly. *I know they are not flirting with me right fucking now.*

One walks over. "Are you Layla Ali?" he asks. I have always been mistaken for her.

"If I say yes, will you tell me what the hell is going on?"

"Stand up!" This comes from a stern-faced white man who acts as if he's heard it all before. He seems to be in charge. They handcuff me. "You are under arrest for grand theft auto." *Black woman handcuffed and sitting on the curb. What the hell?*

The detectives interview me. Knowing I haven't done anything illegal, I figure they will let me go quickly. Instead, they hold me for over an hour of questioning. They keep showing me pictures of people I've never seen in my life, insisting I know them.

I give them Anthony's name, and tell them to get his ass up there. For some reason, they refuse to call him. I can't understand this. They keep trying to convince me that even if I am telling the truth and I'm not involved, my boyfriend will abandon me to take the fall for him.

All the mug shots they show me are of black men. They don't know that my boyfriend is an Italian boy from Europe. Finally, they let me call Anthony from the police department phone while they stand and watch me. He never answers blocked numbers, but for some reason, he does this time.

"Listen to me clearly. I was arrested for grand theft auto, and you need to come get me out of this mess right now." He sounds confused but agrees to come as soon as possible. They hand me an orange jumpsuit, fingerprint me, and say that if I'm not bailed out within four hours, I'll be transferred to Los Angeles County Jail.

They put me in a cell, and I start to panic. The walls are so close that I can touch both sides when I stretch out my arms. The toilet is stainless steel, and the bed is made of concrete and has only a thin mattress. *Maybe if I put the blanket over my head and sleep, I can stop the panic that's brewing inside of me. No, nothing is working. I can't breathe. Inhale, exhale. Inhale, exhale. Maybe if I sit at this concrete slab they're calling a desk and try reading a magazine.*

I cover my head and start singing a hymn…*Jesus loves me, this I know… for the Bible tells me so…yes, Jesus loves me…yes, Jesus loves me…yes, Jesus loves me, for the Bible tells me so…* It's helping a little bit. My heart rate is slowing down.

~ ~ ~

Hours go by and no sign of Anthony. I'm starting to think the detectives are right. I hit the intercom about six times, inquiring about my release. The female officer is so mean, she threatens to do something to me if I do not stop hitting the button. Finally, the guard tells me that Anthony is here and is going through the procedure to bail me out.

Two more hours pass, but I'm still locked in. Then finally the door opens. I'm given my clothes and released. I am so happy to see Anthony that I have no time to be angry. I hug him and ask him to tell me what the hell is going on.

Anthony explains that he showed the detectives the eighty-thousand-dollar contract between him and his broker—a guy he hired to find the cars (his

and mine). He also shows them copies of checks proving that he paid the car notes. After seeing all this, the detectives finally realize that we were the victims of a scam and not the perpetrators. Of course, this doesn't stop them from keeping my Benz and recommending that Anthony turn his in. He does.

Yes, he's the victim, but is he really? How long had he known these people? And if he didn't know them, why would he do a deal with them? The people in the photos I saw all looked like criminals. Are these people Anthony is working with?

~ ~ ~

Some bad gangster guy claims he lost over sixty-five-thousand dollars with Anthony, and was demanding some kind of collateral as payment. So Anthony gave him something he did not own. Now, Gangster Guy Number Two, who does own the thing Anthony gave as collateral, is here at Anthony's office to get it back. The only problem is, Anthony can't get his hands on the collateral until he comes up with sixty-five-thousand dollars to pay Gangster Guy Number One.

This is really getting scary. I thought being with him would be different, but he's involved with things far worse than I could have imagined.

Anthony and I are pulling into the carport when two men approach us, one on his side and the other on mine. I have a sinking feeling in my stomach, but Anthony hops out and greets them warmly. I get out and immediately go to the door that leads into the office. As I do, I notice that the guy on my side is standing a little farther back, right at the rear of the bumper. His hands are in gloves. That's odd. I also notice that he's wearing a black leather jacket—in the summertime.

I let the door close behind me, trying to act as if I have no sense that anything's wrong. But as soon as the door closes, I'm running up the stairs to tell whoever is here what's happening. It's way after hours and no one is here. They're all gone for the day. I go to the balcony that's just above the driveway and listen quietly. I'm so shaky.

I'm up on the fourth floor in our office bedroom, planning my escape. *Damn, I'm so high up. But I've got to get out of here.* I hop over the balcony to the next one and then to the next until I get to the edge and to the ladder on the side of the building. With only my cell phone in my hand, I run to the gym next door and call Mama, who begs me to get away and call the police.

I don't quite know the situation, so I can't do that. Instead, I climb back up onto the balcony the same way I climbed down and return to the bedroom, where I can hear their voices. They're in the house now.

I'm at the edge of the stairs. The man who was on Anthony's side of the car looks up and sees me. It seems that he's counting the number of people in the building. I'm so nervous. I listen to the conversation while keeping my eyes on the balcony. If I hear anything, I'll lock the door and go back to the ladder.

The man with the gloves says loudly, "Get away from him. He's done a lot of bad things to a lot of people, and they're all after him." And they both leave. My heart is still beating fast.

Anthony has no idea that I just scaled over three balconies and ran across a parking entrance to get to the gym. He tries to explain what's happening but I have no interest in anything he's saying. I'm getting off this crazy ride before I get hurt for something I'm not even involved in. But, of course, if you're the girlfriend, you're already involved. So I'm watching my back. The fear makes it hard to sleep but I finally drift off.

I now realize that Anthony is also dealing in the streets—and has no street sense. I can no longer respect him like I did before the incident. Small details begin to emerge that contradict what he has told me about his financial state. He says he's a millionaire, and I've seen a bank statement that proves it. I now believe he's committing white-collar crimes. The money is in and then it is out—and that's exactly where I'm getting ready to be.

~ ~ ~

Watching Anthony take his clothes out of my coat closet and drive off is a relief. I did not get invested in him. *Thank you, God, for that extra forty-two thousand dollars that he put in my account for rent. With my history with men, I knew this shit was not going to last.* I'm about one month away from that money being gone. I haven't even touched the hundred and fifty thousand dollars. I didn't have to—he took care of everything. The only money coming out of my pocket was the money I gave Mama every month to help out with food.

I have to be smart about this. The rent is thirty-five hundred dollars a month, plus my car note on the BMW. (Thankfully, I kept my BMW even after Anthony bought me the Benz.) Then, there's insurance, gas bill, electric, food, and entertainment. That's a little shy of six thousand a month. Man, I am going to miss that cushion he was giving me. Back to reality. Okay, $6,000 a month for 12 months…that's $72,000, leaving me $78,000.

That gives me only two years here if I don't do any other spending. No, that is not going to work. I need to get into a cheaper apartment and get another job, or sign another contract or something. I will never be hungry or homeless again. The stupidest thing I did was quit my job. But this time, I thought I had things set up right. I thought I'd covered myself. I thought I might get another year out of him. Damn, that's harsh to say. I know it is. Poor boy didn't know what he was getting himself into. I guess I didn't either. I have no more love inside to give to a man. I actually did him a favor by putting him out. I've said goodbye to another man.

~ ~ ~

I take a much needed break to reflect upon why I feel I need a man so badly and if it's still important that I have one. In order to regroup, I am willing to remove myself from the business of music for a while. What I can't bring myself to do is let go of family, even if they've caused the most pain.

14

I Am Not God
(Relieve Me of My Duties)

"Family:

• A fundamental social group in society typically

consisting of one or two parents and their children.

• Two or more people who share goals and values, have long-term commitments to one another, and reside usually in the same dwelling.

• A group of persons related by blood."

(Webster's Dictionary)

Mama is helping Nia deal with some kind of mental breakdown. I'm so proud of Mama. She hasn't taken street drugs in years, and last year she even stopped drinking.

But today, she's feeling sick and is complaining about stomach pains. I realize I need to get her to a hospital right away. As we sit in the emergency room, things go from bad to worse. Mama is vomiting up green stuff nonstop.

"What is that?" I ask the nurse, but she won't tell me. It looks like poison. Radiologists push Mama into an MRI, believing the vomiting is connected to gallbladder malfunction.

The test proves as much. Mama's gallbladder is inflamed, and they need to admit her for further tests. The pain is so severe that she's buckling, but no one can do anything for her until the doctor arrives in the morning.

I go back to her house to sleep, but I keep one eye open the whole night, waiting for the clock to hit 7:00 a.m. so I can be with her. I return to find Mama in severe pain. Under a hospital robe, she's still wearing her sweats from the night before. The pain, she says, is almost crippling. She can only lie on one side. I'm in the process of trying to sit her up in a chair when Mama feels sick. I quietly grab a bucket, and she immediately vomits up dark blood. I can't believe my eyes.

"Help her!" I scream. "Please help her!" The nurses rush in to do whatever they can, but it keeps coming. I feel like I'm about to faint. I splash water on my face, but it doesn't work. My heart is beating so fast that I can't breathe. I have to sit down.

Mama finally stops vomiting, and the nurses bring the surgeon in to talk to me. He explains that he'll be performing an emergency operation to take out her gallbladder, which is so gangrenous that it has died and poisoned her system. It's become septic, as he calls it. Normal white-blood-cell levels range between four thousand and eleven thousand. Mama's levels have skyrocketed to fifty thousand.

The nurses prepare Mama for surgery. I saw the fear in her eyes when she was throwing up blood. Mama is so drained from pain that she wants them to take her gallbladder out.

Grandma joins me, and we wait several hours for a progress report. We console each other as we wait. My grandmother is rather frail, so I'm afraid this ordeal might cause more stress than she can bear. I hold it together for her when all I really want to do is curl up in a ball and not say a word. Finally, the surgeon walks into the room, and it feels like everything goes into slow motion before he actually reaches us.

"Your mother made me work hard," he says, looking tired from the operation. He shows us a picture of the gallbladder he just removed. It's supposed to be a light-bluish color, but hers is as black as tar. He tells us that he got it all out but that Mama is still very sick and is receiving a high dosage of antibiotics.

~ ~ ~

It's been twelve days since Mama's operation, and I've left the hospital only once to pack a bag of necessities for her. At this point, Nia is living with Mama, and when I get to the house, she is there. "Did she die? Is she dead?" she asks, in a very aggressive voice.

"No, she is not dead," I say. I am confused and angered by her behavior. "Why is she not dead?" she asks, as if she is disappointed that Mama is still alive.

I tell her she better get the hell away from me before I kill her.

Mama is scheduled for a second surgery. She has a leak in her stomach where bile is seeping in. Every day, we pray that the little plastic bottle attached to her side will stop filling up with brownish gunk. We hoped that this gunk was only the water they were using to flush out her system. But no, it's a leak for sure. The doctors put in a small stint to shut off the leak. This surgery, an endoscopic retrograde ERCP, carries several risks—a pancreatic infection being one of the worst.

The worst happens. Mama is now suffering from a pancreatic infection in addition to the original infection from her gallbladder. She fights for her life for another ten days until we get a miracle from God himself. She's being released from the hospital today with her blood count back to normal. Hallelujah!

~ ~ ~

After being out of the hospital for two weeks, Mama's condition has vastly improved. But today she complains that her stomach is hurting as much as it did before the first surgery. We give it a couple of days, and then we return to the hospital to find that her blood count has shot up again.

"She's infected from head to toe," the doctors tell us. *Oh, my God!*

Since this illness struck her, I've acquired an education in infections. This one carries a ninety-percent mortality rate, which means that only about ten percent of its victims survive. Now she's been hit again, twice within a two-week span. *Can Mama endure and fight this off once more?*

For the next eleven days, I sleep next to Mama in a rollaway bed. Thank God I'm here. I don't want to bad-mouth the nurses, but Mama has to relieve herself about every two hours, and if I weren't here to lift her and put the bedpan under her, who knows what a mess it would be? The nurses never get here in time. Mama presses the button for immediate help, but they never appear for at least fifteen minutes.

I stay here not only because I'm worried, but also because if I leave, Mama will not receive adequate care. She has massage pads strapped to her legs to keep her from clotting, so she's unable to get to the bathroom quickly. Thus, she has to rely on bedpans, not to mention the bucket I grab every time the strong antibiotics running though her veins make her puke. If I weren't here, she'd have puked and pissed all over herself many times.

An infection specialist monitors her progress, but all they can really do is treat her with antibiotics and wait. Finally, her blood count returns to normal, and they're able to release her. Mama has beaten the odds once again. I can't help but admire her bravery and strength through it all.

Her illness has taken its toll on me as well. During the entire stretch, I've been completely stressed out, and I've never slept longer than two hours at a time. I'm worn out—whipped from fighting my mother's battles. I have my own issues to overcome. It's a wonder I'm still standing. I pray to God to keep his hands on her so I can look after my own life.

~ ~ ~

After pleading and prayers from the family, Nia is now seeing a therapist who might be able to help her deal with her demons and let go of them. She slowly seems to be returning to the person I knew. She even tells Mama about the molestation.

Mama's boyfriend died three years ago. So when Nia told Mama, she was initially angry with her for waiting until he had died to tell her. In anger, she told Nia she should have just kept it to herself. She took his death hard, and now she doesn't know whether to love him or hate him. She wants answers from him. A few weeks later, after the anger subsides, Mama sobs in shock and disbelief.

The three of us have had our fair share of dark days, with various levels of abuse we are still fighting. And although there is still much to do, I'm happy to say that we are all survivors.

My sister has had so much bottled up inside her for years. And she hasn't had the outlets I've had to help her cope. I have my music and writing. I pray for my sister's full recovery. I pray that she gets her mind, strength, life, and spirit back. I pray that her full recovery becomes the key to getting her daughter back in her life.

~ ~ ~

Okay, so now what? Early this morning, I look in the bathroom mirror of my new, less expensive apartment. I see a face I feel I'm seeing for the first time. Now what? What happens now that Mama and my past don't have the same hold on me…now that I've turned those things over to God?

I've had a lot of time to think since being in the hospital with Mama. We sometimes take a beating in life, but what I realize is that we're built to be resilient. We're built to withstand physical and mental abuse. And some of us are lucky enough to come out of it with our right minds and beating hearts.

Mama taught me something extremely valuable throughout all these years of feeling that the roles were reversed, that I was the mother and she was the child. She taught me about inner strength, about willpower—mine and hers. By putting me into a position where I was constantly having to take care of her, I learned how strong I really am and how much willpower I possess.

While the roles were reversed, I never noticed Mama's strong inner core. It never occurred to me that even during the years when she was dealing with an active addiction, she never stopped being a stickler about the things she felt were important for Nia's and my future. She made sure we always went to school, that we had good manners and were respectful to our elders, that we weren't living too fast.

When Mama went into the hospital and was fighting for her life without showing any fear, and without complaining, I finally understood how strong she really was—and how strong she had been from the very beginning. If it had been me in that hospital bed going through that, I might have died. I didn't think she would be strong enough to handle it, but she did.

God answered my prayers in that hospital. I asked God to give me a sign so I would feel comfortable letting her go and giving her to him. And it happened—God showing me that Mama was strong enough to survive was the sign I was asking for. For the first time, I was able to clearly see Mama's strength.

Now it's time I do something to secure my financial independence. I search my contacts. There has to be someone in here that owes me a favor. I've loaned so much money out, paying other people's rents and buying groceries. Now it's my turn to ask for help.

Then it hits me. I can't keep looking to someone else to jumpstart my engine. I have to stabilize my life myself, piece by piece, part by part. So many people in this life get stuck in yesterday to the point where they can't change and grow into tomorrow. I don't want that to be me.

My friend tells me they're hiring at the Peninsula Hotel in Beverly Hills. I'll apply today—right now. *I don't have hospitality experience but I'm a people person, so how hard can it be?*

Sharply dressed in a black, crepe, Zelda pantsuit I still have from my Ames Apparel days, I'm now going through my fourth round of interviews at the Peninsula.

"You're hired," the manager tells me, "but only for the holidays. We'll see how it goes." They'll pay me fifteen dollars an hour to host at the Belvedere, the main restaurant in the hotel.

This is a super conservative hotel—and there's not that much color in this place. I'm one of only two, and they put both of us up at the front door. I guess they feel they need some brown sugar.

We entertain many VIPs, and we have to be very discreet. I see just about everyone. I personally seat a legendary British actor every day at seven-thirty in the morning for breakfast. I always have everything ready for him when he comes in: patio seating with a newspaper, two chairs, and black napkins. He always has egg whites, coffee, and toast. He is surprisingly gracious. It's not that I should expect anything less, but I just can't believe how nice and approachable he is, especially to me. He sees me so much now that he greets me with a warm smile each day and says goodbye with a kiss on the cheek.

It's humbling working here at the Peninsula because you never know who you'll run into. One day, a VP of Atlantic Records walks in and sees me standing at the post, waiting to seat him. Until now, he's only seen me in a power position, hard-balling him on a contract. *But what am I to do? Run every time*

I see an old business contact? No. I have to stand proud, do what I'm here to do, and excel at it.

~ ~ ~

The holidays come and go and it is the last day of work for me. Although they have grown to love me, the restaurant has no place to put me. They're already taking hours away from some of their full-time employees.

One of my VIPs is very unhappy to hear that I'm leaving. He goes out of his way to talk to the general manager, but there's nothing they can do. The VIP has been dining here for twenty years and has a lot of influence. Unfortunately, the economy has a bigger influence on this particular decision.

He makes a couple of calls on my behalf to two restaurants owned by celebrity chefs—Spago of Beverly Hills, owned by Wolfgang Puck, and Bouchon, owned by Thomas Kelly. *A wealthy white man sees something in me and wants only to help? This is a different experience for me.* He says he's watched me work very hard, catering to everyone's needs, and he would like to return the favor.

I interview with both restaurants, and both of them offer me a job. It's a blessing. In this economy, where some can't even find one job, I'm offered two. Before I got the job offers, I had a lot of time on my hands to think about all the bad experiences in my life, and all the struggles in my family. Now, someone does something for me out of the kindness of his heart, and his kind gesture results in not one job but two. It is a humbling experience.

I have to take both jobs. I work at Bouchon five days a week and at Spago three days. I work sixteen-hour days sometimes, but I don't complain. This is my second chance to stand on my own feet, and that is exactly what I will do. I haven't given up on my dreams.

I don't get off work and put my feet up. I'm making films now, and Tiny and I are back together, making music. We reunite with Slim from Nsomnia Kafe (she now goes by the name Slim Good), and launch our new single and video. It does well on YouTube. Not bad for some old broads.

In my life, I have experienced some rotten times, but through it all, I've managed to find sweet moments. Those moments have turned into days, weeks, and now months. Something has changed in me. I no longer see the dark cloud. I believe it was there because I always anticipated terrible things and therefore manifested them. I did not believe true happiness was out there for me—a girl with a pimp for a father and a mother who was a victim of the fast life. But they were much more than that, weren't they?

My father was a star athlete who cared for his family. Who wanted to make his father proud. He had his own demons because he made a decision that altered his life.

Mama never stopped loving me. She never stopped wanting the best for me. She was always present, guiding us, trying to instill valuable things in us, even when she was under the influence of alcohol or drugs. Her display of strength was delayed but right on time.

Do I admire them in some strange way? Yes, today I know that I do. They are both still standing and trying to be better people. My father is now trying to have a relationship with all of his children. I have heard there are twenty-six of us. I have not met them all, but I've met more than a third of them. It is my mission to find and meet them all.

My eldest brother gets in touch with me and asks if I will participate in a siblings reunion without our father included. He rounds up a great amount of them, so I agree. We learn a lot about each other at that reunion. Some who did not grow up with him hear from those who did, and find peace. Some almost feel grateful that they didn't grow up with this sometimes-horrible man. We even find things in common.

The feeling of abandonment is the most obvious consensus, even among the ones I call the royal seven—the seven who spent the most time with him. What surprises us the most is that he signed all our birth certificates, which means he was there when we were each born. He cared enough to make sure to claim us. That speaks volumes to us and gives me some peace.

~ ~ ~

I still don't know exactly what my purpose is in life. I realize that my biggest problem is fear—fear of being alone, of not being successful, of being stuck in the circumstance, or of not feeling smart enough to make things happen on my own.

What happened to that kid, the wilderness girl, who snared those two birds with the homemade bird catcher? What happened to the kid who wanted to be a superstar or an adventurer exploring the world? She felt like she could conquer the world, but the world proved itself to be unconquerable.

I have extraordinary strength. I also have to contend with the cards I was dealt in this life. But there are fifty-two cards in every deck, and I'm calling for a re-shuffle and a new deal. I'm ready for my second chance, ready to let go of all the facades, ready to be vulnerable—an open book. At last, I am content being Billie Raquel King, the little girl from Compton.

Afterword

I am happy to report that I have a newfound sense of freedom and I'm living in my true calling as a writer. Whether I am writing songs, screenplays or books, I know that the reason I am able to do so is because my soul has finally found some peace; this allows me to live up to my full potential.

My mother and I couldn't be closer. She has always truly been the love of my life. I see her at least three times a week and speak to her every day. We have a rule—we say a 10:00 a.m. good morning and a 10:00 p.m. good night. She has been drug free for a few years now, but still has an occasional cocktail or two.

The hard living has taken a toll on her, and she is dealing with some health conditions, like fibromyalgia and knee and hip problems. But I am always there to assist her when needed and I wouldn't have it any other way.

My sister Nia is doing a lot better. She lives alone in an apartment and we see her a couple of times a week. She is on medication now to help with depression, and has reverted to the soft-spoken person I remember as a child. Her eldest daughter is in college and still lives with Mama. Her baby girl, who is now five, lives with her father, and Mama still has her every other weekend.

I still worry about Mama but not as much. I have learned that you can't save someone who doesn't want to be saved—or even feel as though they need saving. My greatest challenge has been to let all of them go and let God.

I realized that trying to save them was killing me. I still struggle with this but I

am working on it every day. We are all doing our best in this big, bad world.

About the Author

Billie King was born and raised in Compton, California, later moving to Los Angeles, and has always been surrounded by entertainment. Living in a city were celebrities pass you on the street daily, and sit next to you in coffee shops, King's fate was written in the stars. It was only a matter of time before she was bitten by the entertainment bug and entered the arena of music at a professional level.

By 1999, she was penning songs for some of R&B's hottest acts. She went on to launch her own record label, earning a spot on Billboard's Top 100, and receiving a couple of gold and platinum plaques. She has encountered, and been privileged to work with, many of the greatest talents in music. In addition to her own considerable talent, she has developed a strong business sense and networking capabilities invaluable to those around her.

Billie has been known to move mountains. It was her gentle, quiet steeliness that allowed her to build a solid discography of work while setting about to conquer the demons of her past. She notes, "Out of the broken glass, and dark streets that obscured my path, I somehow managed to live my dreams out loud. Now, I find myself contemplating my back story and putting together the pieces of my life."

King lives and records in Southern California. When she is not in the studio or out in the music scene, she spends her time writing screenplays and engaging in her meditation practice.